Hamlyn Kitchen Shelf

BAKING
AT HOME

Christian Teubner

Hamlyn
London · New York · Sydney · Toronto

This edition published by
The Hamlyn Publishing Group Limited
London · New York · Sydney · Toronto
Astronaut House, Feltham, Middlesex, England
© Copyright The Hamlyn Publishing Group Limited 1982

ISBN 0 600 32283 1

First published under the title
Back-Vergnugen leicht gemacht
© Copyright by Gräfe und Unzer Verlag, München
Some of these recipes have appeared in *The Best of Cooking*
and *The Best of Baking*, published by The Hamlyn
Publishing Group Limited.

Set in 10 on 10½pt Monophoto Sabon 669
by Tameside Filmsetting Ltd,
Ashton-under-Lyne, Lancashire
Printed in Italy

Contents

Useful facts and figures

Notes on metrication

In this book quantities are given in metric and Imperial measures. Exact conversion from Imperial to metric measures does not usually give very convenient working quantities and so the metric measures have been rounded off into units of 25 grams. The table below shows the recommended equivalents.

Ounces	Approx g to nearest whole figure	Recommended conversion to nearest unit of 25
1	28	25
2	57	50
3	85	75
4	113	100
5	142	150
6	170	175
7	198	200
8	227	225
9	255	250
10	283	275
11	312	300
12	340	350
13	368	375
14	396	400
15	425	425
16 (1 lb)	454	450
17	482	475
18	510	500
19	539	550
20 ($1\frac{1}{4}$ lb)	567	575

Note: When converting quantities over 20 oz first add the appropriate figures in the centre column, then adjust to the nearest unit of 25. As a general guide, 1 kg (1000 g) equals 2.2 lb or about 2 lb 3 oz. This method of conversion give good results in nearly all cases, although in certain pastry and cake recipes a more accurate conversion is necessary to produce a balanced recipe.

Liquid measures The millilitre has been used in this book and the following table gives a few examples.

Imperial	Approx ml to nearest whole figure	Recommended ml
$\frac{1}{4}$ pint	142	150 ml
$\frac{1}{2}$ pint	283	300 ml
$\frac{3}{4}$ pint	425	450 ml
1 pint	567	600 ml
$1\frac{1}{2}$ pint	851	900 ml
$1\frac{3}{4}$ pints	992	1000 ml (1 litre)

Spoon measures All spoon measures given in this book are level unless otherwise stated.

Can sizes At present, cans are marked with the exact (usually to the nearest whole number) metric equivalent of the Imperial weight of the contents, so we have followed this practice when giving can sizes.

Oven temperatures
The table below gives recommended equivalents.

	°C	°F	Gas Mark
Very cool	110	225	$\frac{1}{4}$
	120	250	$\frac{1}{2}$
Cool	140	275	1
	150	300	2
Moderate	160	325	3
	180	350	4
Moderately hot	190	375	5
	200	400	6
Hot	220	425	7
	230	450	8
Very hot	240	475	9

Note: WHEN MAKING ANY OF THE RECIPES IN THIS BOOK, ONLY FOLLOW ONE SET OF MEASURES AS THEY ARE NOT INTERCHANGEABLE.

Introduction

There is nothing quite so inviting as the mouth-watering aroma of freshly baked bread or cakes. Hot from the oven and neatly laid out to cool, the tempting goodies must be one of the most satisfying sights to adorn the kitchen table.

Baking at Home offers a wide range of exciting recipes for the cook who is prepared to devote a little extra time to achieve perfect results. In presenting these recipes, Christian Teubner brings home to us the true delights of baking day, introducing many ideas from his German homeland as well as other traditional favourites from all over the world. Recipes for yeast bakes, pastries and puffs, small cakes and biscuits, family cakes and luscious cream gâteaux are all included.

A chapter on baking with yeast presents not only recipes for simple savoury breads, but an interesting selection of sweet breads and yeast cakes. For example, Almond twist, Hazelnut stollen and a deliciously rich Garland cake filled with fruit, nuts and chocolate and topped with a thin rum icing add variety to your baking, and you will find seasonal recipes for Easter bread and a delightfully decorated Santa Claus bread. Ideas are also included for traditional favourites such as Jam doughnuts and Danish pastries and exciting suggestions for a Cream cheese crumble cake, Plum slice or Crisp butter squares.

In the chapters that follow special emphasis has been laid on extending basic recipes to provide a selection of dishes which are suitable for all occasions – savouries for family snacks or meals, dinners and parties; short-crust, puff and choux pastries for simple desserts as well as elaborately decorated gâteaux. In the recipes the method outlines each stage of creaming, whisking and folding in the ingredients, and with a little practice in perfecting the techniques you will produce excellent results every time. The superb colour photographs will encourage you to experiment and offer you guidance in completing the decorative finishing touches.

Don't forget that breads, cakes and biscuits are ideal candidates for the freezer – they should be cooled and frozen before being filled and iced. Many of the yeast cakes and breads can be sliced before freezing, making it easy to remove just one or two slices at a time. Home-baked rolls or bread, or a slice of rich yeast cake, will liven up any lunch-box snack, and it requires no extra effort when your freezer is well stocked with such treats.

You will find the breads, cakes and biscuits, pastries and gâteaux in *Baking at Home* deliciously different and worthy of being served time and time again. It is hoped that you will gain as much pleasure in cooking from these recipes as your family and friends will in sampling the dishes.

Baking with yeast

Onion tart

Cooking temperature moderately hot
(200 C, 400 F, Gas 6)
Cooking time 45 minutes

300 g/11 oz strong plain flour
1 teaspoon salt
20 g/¾ oz fresh yeast or 2 teaspoons dried yeast
125 ml/4 fl oz lukewarm milk
50 g/2 oz butter
1 egg, lightly beaten
FILLING
50 g/2 oz streaky bacon
2 tablespoons oil
450 g/1 lb onions, sliced
3 eggs
salt and pepper
2 teaspoons caraway seeds
150 ml/¼ pint soured cream

Lightly grease a 30-cm/12-in loose-bottomed flan tin. Sift the flour and salt into a bowl making a hollow in the centre. Cream the yeast with a little of the milk, add the remaining milk and pour it into the middle of the flour. Sprinkle a little flour over the surface of the yeast liquid and leave it in a warm place for 15 minutes. Alternatively, if using dried yeast, pour the milk into the middle of the flour and sprinkle over the yeast. Stir it lightly into the milk, then leave it in a warm place until frothy.

Melt the butter, add it to the yeast liquid together with the egg and stir into the dry ingredients to form a dough. Knead the dough thoroughly for 10 minutes until smooth. Place it in a lightly oiled bowl, cover and allow the dough to rise for 30–40 minutes. Knead it lightly and roll out evenly into a circle large enough to line the prepared flan tin. Line the tin and trim the edges. Prick the base all over with a fork to avoid bubbles forming during baking.

To make the filling, cut the rind off and chop the bacon finely. Heat the oil, add the bacon and onions, and fry them until lightly browned. Allow to cool slightly. Beat the eggs with a generous sprinkling of seasoning, the caraway seeds and cream. Place the onions in the dough case, spreading them evenly over the base, then slowly pour in the egg mixture. Bake the tart in a moderately hot oven (200 C, 400 F, Gas 6) for 45 minutes until golden brown, set and thoroughly cooked.

Spicy tomato pizza

Cooking temperature moderate
(180 C, 350 F, Gas 4)
Cooking time 40–45 minutes

225 g/8 oz strong plain flour
½ teaspoon salt
15 g/½ oz fresh yeast or 1½ teaspoons dried yeast
150 ml/¼ pint lukewarm milk
4 tablespoons olive oil
1 egg yolk
freshly ground black pepper
TOPPING
350 g/12 oz ripe tomatoes
1 onion
8 stuffed green olives
50 g/2 oz salami, thinly sliced
salt and pepper
½ teaspoon dried oregano
100 g/4 oz mozzarella cheese, thinly sliced

Grease a large baking tray. Sift the flour and salt into a bowl, making a hollow in the centre. Cream the yeast with a little of the milk, add the remaining milk and pour it into the middle of the flour. Sprinkle a little flour over the surface of the yeast liquid and leave it in a warm place for 15 minutes. Alternatively, if using dried yeast, pour the milk into the middle of the flour and sprinkle over the yeast. Stir it lightly into the milk, then leave it in a warm place until frothy.

Stir half the olive oil and egg yolk into the yeast liquid together with a generous sprinkling of pepper. Beat the yeast liquid into the dry ingredients to form a dough. Knead it thoroughly for 10 minutes then allow the dough to rest, covered, in an oiled bowl in a warm place for 30 minutes. Knead lightly and roll it out into a 35-cm/14-in round. Place the dough base on the baking tray and prick it all over with a fork. Thinly slice the tomatoes, onions and olives. Arrange the salami, onion and tomatoes over the base. Top with the olives, seasoning and oregano and cover with the cheese. Sprinkle the olive oil over the pizza and bake in a moderate oven (180 C, 350 F, Gas 4) for 40–45 minutes until golden brown and bubbling. Serve immediately.

Top: Spicy tomato pizza; *Bottom:* Onion tart

Bread sticks

Cooking temperature hot
(220 C, 425 F, Gas 7)
Cooking time 8–12 minutes

350 g/12 oz strong plain flour
½ teaspoon salt
100 g/4 oz butter
15 g/½ oz fresh yeast or 1½ teaspoons dried yeast
3 tablespoons lukewarm milk
2 eggs, lightly beaten
egg yolk to glaze
coarse salt and caraway seeds

Grease a baking tray. Sift the flour and salt into a bowl, add the butter, cut in small flakes, and rub it into the flour until the mixture resembles fine breadcrumbs. Cream the yeast with the lukewarm milk and allow it to stand in a warm place for about 10 minutes. Stir the eggs with the yeast liquid into the flour to make a stiff dough. Knead thoroughly for 10 minutes then place it in an oiled bowl, cover it and leave in a warm place for 15 minutes. Break off 25-g/1-oz pieces of dough and roll them into 1-cm/½-in thick sticks measuring approximately 15 cm/6 in in length. Place these on the prepared baking tray, brush them with a little egg yolk and sprinkle a little coarse salt or caraway seeds on top. Bake the sticks in a hot oven (220 C, 425 F, Gas 7) for 8–12 minutes until they are golden brown. Cool them on a wire rack and serve these bread sticks with tall glasses of chilled lager.

Variation
Sesame seeds or a little grated Parmesan cheese can be substituted for the coarse salt or caraway seeds. The bread sticks may be served warm with a light first course or luncheon dish.

Bavarian rolls

Cooking temperature hot
(220 C, 425 F, Gas 7)
Cooking time 30–40 minutes

100 g/4 oz butter, melted to coat the baking tin
450 g/1 lb strong plain flour
1 teaspoon salt
40 g/1½ oz fresh yeast or 4½ teaspoons dried yeast
250 ml/8 fl oz lukewarm milk
50 g/2 oz butter, melted
50 g/2 oz caster sugar
2 eggs, lightly beaten
grated rind of ½ lemon

Coat a small roasting tin or a 23 × 15-cm/9 × 6-in shallow oblong tin with all the melted butter. Sift the flour and salt into a bowl, making a hollow in the centre. Cream the yeast with a little of the milk, add the remaining milk and pour it into the middle of the flour. Sprinkle a little flour over the surface of the yeast liquid and leave it in a warm place for 15 minutes. Alternatively, if using dried yeast, pour the milk into the middle of the flour and sprinkle over the yeast. Stir it lightly into the milk, then leave it in a warm place until frothy.

Mix the butter with the sugar, eggs and lemon rind, add to the yeast liquid, then gradually stir in the flour to make a dough. Knead the dough thoroughly for 10 minutes then place in an oiled bowl, cover it with cling film and leave it to rise in a warm place for 40 minutes. Lightly knead the dough and divide it into 50-g/2-oz portions, forming each into a ball and rolling these in the melted butter in the tin. Arrange them next to each other, cover with oiled cling film and leave the rolls to rise for 30–40 minutes. Bake them in a hot oven (220 C, 425 F, Gas 7) for 40 minutes until well risen and golden brown. Turn out and cool on a wire rack.

Suitable for freezing: The cooled rolls may be frozen and stored for 2–3 months. They may be reheated from frozen in a cool oven and served warm.

Top: Bavarian rolls;
Bottom: Plum slice (page 27)

Spiced bread

**Cooking temperature hot
(220 C, 425 F, Gas 7)
Cooking time 20–25 minutes**

450 g/1 lb strong plain flour
1 teaspoon salt
40 g/1½ oz fresh yeast or 4½ teaspoons dried
yeast
250 ml/8 fl oz lukewarm milk
2 eggs, lightly beaten
1 teaspoon caraway seeds
1 teaspoon ground coriander
½ teaspoon aniseeds
¼ teaspoon ginger
egg yolk to glaze
TOPPING (*optional*)
2 tablespoons coarse salt
1 tablespoon caraway seeds

Grease three baking trays. Sift the flour and salt into a bowl, making a hollow in the centre. Cream the yeast with a little of the milk, add the remaining milk and pour it into the middle of the flour. Sprinkle a little flour over the surface of the yeast liquid and leave it in a warm place for 15 minutes. Alternatively, if using dried yeast, pour the milk into the middle of the flour and sprinkle over the yeast. Stir it lightly into the milk, then leave it in a warm place until frothy.

Stir the eggs, caraway seeds, ground coriander, aniseeds and ginger into the yeast liquid and stir in the dry ingredients to make a dough. Knead it thoroughly for 10 minutes then place it in an oiled bowl, cover and leave the dough to rise in a warm place for 30–40 minutes. Knead the bread lightly and divide it into three equal portions. Shape each into a round flat or long oval loaf. Place the loaves on the prepared baking trays, cover with oiled cling film and allow to rise in a warm place for 20–30 minutes.

Whisk the egg yolk with a tablespoon of water and use it to brush the loaves. Sprinkle with the salt and caraway seeds (if liked) and bake the bread in a hot oven (220 C, 425 F, Gas 7) for 20–25 minutes until crisp and browned.

Variation

Coriander bread: Use wholemeal flour instead of white flour and leave out the caraway seeds and aniseeds. Shape the dough into two long loaves and sprinkle the top with whole coriander instead of the salt and caraway seeds. Continue as above.

Party rolls

**Cooking temperature hot
(220 C, 425 F, Gas 7)
Cooking time 15–20 minutes**

450 g/1 lb strong plain flour
1 teaspoon salt
40 g/1½ oz fresh yeast or 4½ teaspoons dried
yeast
250 ml/8 fl oz lukewarm milk
50 g/2 oz butter
1 egg, lightly beaten
generous pinch each of pepper and nutmeg
egg yolk to glaze
TOPPING
2 tablespoons poppy seeds
2 tablespoons caraway seeds

Lightly grease a baking tray. Sift the flour and salt into a bowl, making a hollow in the centre. Cream the yeast with a little of the milk, add the remaining milk and pour it into the middle of the flour. Sprinkle a little flour over the surface of the yeast liquid and leave it in a warm place for 15 minutes. Alternatively, if using dried yeast, pour the milk into the middle of the flour and sprinkle over the yeast. Stir it lightly into the milk, then leave it in a warm place until frothy.

Melt the butter and stir it into the yeast liquid together with the egg, pepper and nutmeg. Stir in the dry ingredients to form a dough and knead it thoroughly for 10 minutes. Place the dough in a lightly oiled bowl, cover and leave it to rise in a warm place for 30–40 minutes.

Knead lightly, then divide the dough into 50-g/2-oz pieces and shape each into a roll. Place them on the prepared baking tray, cover with oiled cling film and leave in a warm place for 15–20 minutes until the rolls are well risen. Whisk the egg yolk with 2 tablespoons water and use it to brush the rolls. Sprinkle half the rolls with poppy seeds and half with caraway seeds. Use a sharp-pointed knife to cut a cross in the top of each roll and bake them in a hot oven (220 C, 425 F, Gas 7) for 15–20 minutes, then cool them on a wire rack.

Top: Party rolls; *Bottom:* Spiced bread

Garland cake

Cooking temperature moderately hot
(200 C, 400 F, Gas 6)
Cooking time 30–35 minutes

450 g/1 lb strong flour
½ teaspoon salt
40 g/1½ oz fresh yeast or 4½ teaspoons dried
yeast
250 ml/8 fl oz lukewarm milk
100 g/4 oz butter, melted
50 g/2 oz sugar
grated rind of ½ lemon
FILLING
50 g/2 oz butter, melted
50 g/2 oz sugar
75 g/3 oz sultanas
75 g/3 oz blanched almonds, coarsely chopped
75 g/3 oz chocolate dots
50 g/2 oz dried figs, chopped
ICING
50 g/2 oz icing sugar, sifted
1–2 tablespoons rum

Sift the flour and salt into a bowl, making a hollow in the centre. Cream the yeast with a little of the milk, add the remaining milk and pour it into the middle of the flour. Sprinkle a little flour over the surface of the yeast liquid and leave it in a warm place for 15 minutes. If using dried yeast, pour the milk into the middle of the flour and sprinkle over the yeast. Stir it lightly into the milk; leave in a warm place until frothy.

Stir the butter, sugar and lemon rind into the yeast liquid and gradually mix in the flour. Knead the dough thoroughly for 10 minutes, then place in a lightly oiled bowl, cover with cling film and leave in a warm place for 15–20 minutes. Lightly knead the dough, then roll it into a rectangle measuring 40 × 50 cm/16 × 20 in. Brush with the butter, sprinkle the filling ingredients over the dough and roll up lightly. Cut the roll in half lengthways and carefully twist the two strips together with the cut edge upwards. Shape the twist in a ring on a greased baking tray, cover and allow it to stand in a warm place for 20–30 minutes. Bake the cake in a moderately hot oven (200 C, 400 F, Gas 6) for 30–35 minutes. Cool on a wire rack.

Beat the rum into the icing sugar until smooth and pour over the cake.

Fresh strawberry savarin

Cooking temperature hot
(220 C, 425 F, Gas 7)
Cooking time 40 minutes

20 g/¾ oz fresh yeast
250 ml/8 fl oz lukewarm milk
350 g/12 oz plain flour
4 eggs
40 g/1½ oz caster sugar
1 tablespoon vanilla sugar
½ teaspoon salt
150 g/5 oz butter or margarine, melted
SYRUP
4 tablespoons rum
6 tablespoons dry white wine
250 ml/8 fl oz water
150 g/5 oz sugar
FILLING
225 g/8 oz strawberries
150 ml/¼ pint double cream
50 g/2 oz caster sugar
1 teaspoon chopped pistachio nuts

Grease a 23-cm/9-in savarin tin and dust it with flour. Cream the yeast with a little of the milk, then add the remaining milk. Sift the flour into a bowl, make a well in the centre and pour in the yeast liquid. Sprinkle with a little of the flour, cover and leave for 15 minutes, until frothy.

Beat the eggs with the sugar until frothy, then mix in the vanilla sugar, salt and melted butter. Add this to the yeast mixture, beating well to an almost pouring consistency. Cover and leave it to rise for 10 minutes. Beat the mixture with a wooden spoon and pour it into the prepared savarin tin. Cover and leave it in a warm place until the mixture almost reaches the top of the tin.

Preheat the oven to hot (220 C, 425 F, Gas 7). Bake the savarin for 40 minutes, then turn it out on to a wire rack.

Heat the rum, white wine, water and sugar until the sugar has dissolved. Simmer for 5 minutes. Place a container underneath the wire rack to catch the syrup, then pour it over the savarin until it is completely absorbed. Place it on a serving plate.

Wash, hull and halve the strawberries. Whip the cream with the sugar until stiff. Place most of the strawberries in the centre of the savarin and pipe the cream over them. Use the remaining strawberries and pistachios as decoration.

Top: Garland cake.
Bottom: Fresh strawberry savarin

Almond twist

Cooking temperature hot
(220 C, 425 F, Gas 7)
Cooking time 25–30 minutes

450 g/1 lb strong plain flour
½ teaspoon salt
40 g/1½ oz fresh yeast or 4½ teaspoons dried
yeast
250 ml/8 fl oz lukewarm milk
50 g/2 oz butter
50 g/2 oz sugar
grated rind of ½ lemon
1 egg, lightly beaten
350 g/12 oz ground almonds
2 tablespoons caster sugar
50 g/2 oz candied lemon peel, finely chopped
2 tablespoons rum
2 egg whites
1–2 tablespoons lemon juice
150 g/5 oz icing sugar, sifted

Sift the flour and salt into a bowl, making a hollow
in the centre. Cream the yeast with a little of the
milk, add the remaining milk and pour it into the
middle of the flour. Sprinkle a little flour over
the surface of the yeast liquid and leave it in a
warm place for 15 minutes. Alternatively, if using
dried yeast, pour the milk into the middle of the
flour and sprinkle over the yeast. Stir it lightly
into the milk, then leave it in a warm place until
frothy.

Melt the butter, add the sugar, lemon rind and
the beaten egg. Pour into the yeast liquid, stir well
and gradually mix in the flour to give a smooth
dough. Knead the dough on a floured work surface for 10 minutes then place it in a lightly oiled
bowl, cover with cling film and allow it to stand
in a warm place for 20–30 minutes. Lightly knead
the dough and roll it out to give a rectangle
measuring 40 × 50 cm/16 × 20 in.

Mix the ground almonds with the caster sugar
and candied peel then mix in the rum and egg
whites until smooth. Spread evenly over the dough
and roll it up from the long side. Cut it in half
lengthways and twist the strips together on a
greased baking tray. Cover and leave in a warm
place for 30 minutes.

Bake the twist in a hot oven (220 C, 425 F, Gas 7)
until golden brown – about 25–30 minutes. Cool
on a wire rack. Beat the lemon juice into the icing
sugar to form a thin icing and pour it over the
twist.

Braided loaf

Cooking temperature hot
(220 C, 425 F, Gas 7)
Cooking time 30–40 minutes

575 g/1¼ lb strong plain flour
½ teaspoon salt
25 g/1 oz fresh yeast or 3 teaspoons dried yeast
250 ml/8 fl oz lukewarm milk
75 g/3 oz butter
75 g/3 oz sugar
2 eggs, lightly beaten
grated rind of ½ lemon
egg yolk to glaze
25 g/1 oz preserving or granulated sugar

Grease a baking tray. Sift the flour and salt into a
bowl, making a hollow in the centre. Cream the
yeast with a little of the milk, add the remaining
milk and pour it into the middle of the flour.
Sprinkle a little flour over the surface of the yeast
liquid and leave it in a warm place for 15 minutes.
Alternatively, if using dried yeast, pour the milk
into the middle of the flour and sprinkle over the
yeast. Stir it lightly into the milk, then leave it in a
warm place until frothy.

Melt the butter, add the sugar, eggs, and lemon
rind and pour into the yeast liquid. Gradually
mix in the flour to form a soft dough. Knead it
thoroughly for 10 minutes, then place in a lightly
oiled bowl and cover it with cling film. Allow the
dough to stand in a warm place for 20–30 minutes,
then knead it lightly.

Halve the dough and divide each half into three
equal portions. Roll each piece into a 40-cm/16-in
long strip. Plait three of these rolls together and
place the plait on the prepared baking tray. Twist
two of the remaining pieces together and place
them on top of the plait. Finally, cut the remaining strip in half and roll each piece out to the
original length of 40 cm/16 in. Twist these together and lay the twist along the top of the loaf.

Cover with lightly oiled cling film and leave it to
stand in a warm place for 30–40 minutes.

Brush the loaf with a little egg yolk and sprinkle
it with preserving or granulated sugar before
baking it in a hot oven (220 C, 425 F, Gas 7) for
35–40 minutes. Cool the bread on a wire rack.

Opposite page, left: Braided loaf; *Right:* Almond twist

Date and almond stollen

Cooking temperature moderately hot
(200 C, 400 F, Gas 6)
Cooking time 1 hour

500 g/1 lb plain flour
25 g/1 oz fresh yeast
250 ml/8 fl oz lukewarm milk
50 g/2 oz caster sugar
2 eggs
150 g/5 oz butter, cut into flakes
50 g/2 oz blanched almonds, chopped
grated rind of 1 lemon
pinch of salt
FILLING
25 g/1 oz cornflour
450 ml/$\frac{3}{4}$ pint milk
1 egg yolk
100 g/4 oz caster sugar
225 g/8 oz cooking dates, finely chopped
15 g/$\frac{1}{2}$ oz butter
ICING
200 g/7 oz icing sugar
1 egg white
juice of 1 lemon
2 tablespoons toasted flaked almonds

Grease a baking tray with butter or margarine. Sift the flour into a bowl and form a well in the centre. Cream the yeast with a little of the milk and add 1 tablespoon of the sugar. Add the remaining milk and pour into the flour. Sprinkle a little flour over it, cover and leave it to stand for 15 minutes in a warm place until frothy. Beat the eggs and mix with the remaining sugar, the butter, almonds, lemon rind and salt. Add to the flour and yeast mixture and knead all the ingredients well for 5–10 minutes, to form a smooth, elastic dough. Cover and leave it to rise in a warm place for 30 minutes.

Blend the cornflour with a little of the milk, the egg yolk and sugar. Bring the dates to the boil in the remaining milk. Stir the milk and dates into the cornflour mixture, then add the butter. Return to the heat and bring to the boil, stirring continuously until thickened. Cool, stirring occasionally to prevent a skin forming.

Lightly knead the dough and roll out to 1 cm/$\frac{1}{2}$ in thick on a floured board. Spread the date mixture evenly over it. Turn both side edges over twice towards the centre and press together. Place on the baking tray and leave for 20 minutes.

Preheat the oven to moderately hot (200 C, 400 F, Gas 6) and bake the stollen for 1 hour. Sift the icing sugar and beat it into the egg white with the lemon juice. Ice the stollen while still warm and sprinkle flaked almonds on to the icing.

Almond stollen

Cooking temperature moderately hot
(200 C, 400 F, Gas 6)
Cooking time 25–30 minutes

450 g/1 lb strong plain flour
$\frac{1}{2}$ teaspoon salt
25 g/1 oz fresh yeast or 3 teaspoons dried yeast
250 ml/8 fl oz lukewarm milk
175 g/6 oz butter
50 g/2 oz caster sugar
100 g/4 oz blanched almonds, chopped
100 g/4 oz chopped candied peel
ICING
50 g/2 oz butter, melted
100 g/4 oz icing sugar

Grease a baking tray. Sift the flour and salt into a bowl, making a hollow in the centre. Cream the yeast with a little of the milk, add the remaining milk and pour it into the middle of the flour. Sprinkle a little flour over the surface of the yeast liquid and leave it in a warm place for 15 minutes. Alternatively, if using dried yeast, pour the milk into the middle of the flour and sprinkle over the yeast. Stir lightly into the milk, then leave it in a warm place until frothy.

Melt the butter and add it to the yeast liquid together with the sugar, almonds and candied peel. Knead the dough thoroughly for 10 minutes, place in a lightly oiled bowl and cover, then leave it in a warm place for 30–40 minutes. Lightly knead the dough and roll it into an oblong measuring approximately 30 × 20 cm/12 × 8 in. The dough should be thinner in the middle than at the ends. Carefully fold the dough almost in half from the longer side and lift it on to the baking tray. Cover with oiled cling film and leave in a warm place for 20–30 minutes or until doubled in size. Bake in a moderately hot oven (200 C, 400 F, Gas 6), cool slightly, then brush with melted butter and sprinkle with the icing sugar.

Top: Date and almond stollen.
Bottom: Almond stollen

Hazelnut stollen

**Cooking temperature hot
(220 C, 425 F, Gas 7)
Cooking time 35–40 minutes**

450 g/1 lb strong plain flour
½ teaspoon salt
25 g/1 oz fresh yeast or 3 teaspoons dried yeast
250 ml/8 fl oz lukewarm milk
75 g/3 oz butter, melted
50 g/2 oz sugar
½ teaspoon vanilla essence
1 egg, lightly beaten
FILLING
225 g/8 oz hazelnuts, roasted and ground
25 g/1 oz candied orange peel, finely chopped
2 tablespoons milk
2 egg whites
75 g/3 oz icing sugar
few drops vanilla essence
ICING
50 g/2 oz apricot jam, warmed and sieved
50 g/2 oz icing sugar
1–2 tablespoons rum

Grease and flour a 1-kg/2-lb loaf tin. Sift the flour and salt into a bowl, making a hollow in the centre. Gradually cream the yeast with the milk and pour it into the middle of the flour. Sprinkle a little flour over the surface of the yeast liquid and leave it in a warm place for 15 minutes. If using dried yeast, pour the milk into the middle of the flour and sprinkle over the yeast. Stir it lightly into the milk, then leave in a warm place until frothy. Add the butter, sugar, vanilla essence and beaten egg. Gradually mix in the flour and knead the dough thoroughly for 10 minutes. Place it in a bowl, cover with cling film and allow to rise in a warm place for 30 minutes.

Mix the hazelnuts, candied peel, 2 tablespoons milk, egg whites, sugar and vanilla and mix well. Lightly knead the dough and roll it into a sheet measuring 20 × 18 cm/8 × 7 in. Spread the nut filling over the dough. Brush the border with a little water and roll up the dough from the shorter side. Place the roll in the tin, cover, and leave it in a warm place until the dough has risen almost to the top of the tin. Cut a 1-cm/½-in slit down the length of the loaf and bake it in a hot oven (220 C, 425 F, Gas 7) for 35–40 minutes. Cool on a wire rack, split side up. Spread the jam over the cake; cool. Sift the icing sugar into a bowl and beat in the rum. Pour this icing over the cake.

Easter bread

(Illustrated on the front cover and opposite page)

**Cooking temperature moderately hot
(190 C, 375 F, Gas 5)
Cooking time 30–40 minutes**

1 kg/2¼ lb plain flour
50 g/2 oz fresh yeast
550 ml/18 fl oz lukewarm milk
200 g/7 oz butter, melted
100 g/4 oz caster sugar
2 eggs
pinch of salt
grated rind of 1 lemon
FRUIT LOAF
100 g/4 oz blanched almonds, chopped
200 g/7 oz candied lemon peel, chopped
300 g/11 oz sultanas
1 tablespoon rum
50 g/2 oz butter, melted
50 g/2 oz sugar
PLAITED WREATH
1 egg yolk, beaten to glaze
50 g/2 oz nibbed almonds (optional)
50 g/2 oz sugar (optional)
2 tablespoons rum (optional)

Sift the flour into a bowl and make a well in the centre. Cream the yeast with a little of the milk then stir in the remaining milk. Pour the mixture into the flour, sprinkle with a little of the flour and leave to stand in a warm place for 15 minutes, until frothy. Pour the melted butter into the yeast liquid and mix with the flour, sugar, eggs, salt and lemon rind, to form a dough. Knead for 5–10 minutes until the dough is smooth and elastic. Leave it to rise for 1 hour in a warm place.

Mix the almonds, candied peel, sultanas and rum together and leave to stand for 30 minutes.

Divide the dough in two and knead each half lightly. Mix one half with the fruit mixture and leave it for 15 minutes.

Form the fruit dough into a loaf, place on a greased baking tray and leave it to stand in a warm place for a further 30 minutes. Cut a cross on the top of the loaf and bake in a moderately hot oven (190 C, 375 F, Gas 5) for 30–40 minutes. Brush the loaf with the butter and dust with sugar.

·Divide the remaining dough into three equal pieces and form them into long strips. Plait these together, form into a wreath and brush it with beaten egg yolk. Mix the almonds, sugar and rum, spread over the wreath and bake as above.

Santa Claus bread

(Illustrated on opposite page)

**Cooking temperature hot
(220 C, 425 F, Gas 7)
Cooking time 20 minutes**

450 g/1 lb strong plain flour
$\frac{1}{4}$ teaspoon salt
25 g/1 oz fresh yeast or 3 teaspoons dried yeast
250 ml/8 fl oz lukewarm milk
500 g/2 oz butter, melted
50 g/2 oz sugar
1 egg, lightly beaten
grated rind of $\frac{1}{2}$ lemon
egg yolk to glaze
DECORATION
blanched almonds, peeled pistachio nuts, silver
dragées, sugared sweets and raisins
ICING
2 teaspoons egg white
50 g/2 oz icing sugar, sifted

Grease a baking tray. Draw and cut out the Santa Claus, preferably using greaseproof paper. Sift the flour and salt into a bowl, making a hollow in the centre. Cream the yeast with a little of the milk, add the remaining milk and pour it into the middle of the flour. Sprinkle a little flour over the surface of the yeast liquid and leave it in a warm place for 15 minutes. Alternatively, if using dried yeast, pour the milk into the middle of the flour and sprinkle over the yeast. Stir it lightly into the milk, then leave it in a warm place until frothy.

Melt the butter, add it to the yeast liquid together with the egg and lemon rind. Stir all the ingredients together to form a dough. Knead the dough thoroughly for 10 minutes until smooth, then place it in an oiled bowl, cover and leave it to rise in a warm place for 30–40 minutes. Roll out the dough to about 1 cm/$\frac{1}{2}$ in thick and, using the paper Santa Claus, cut out the dough figures and place them on the baking tray. Leave them in a warm place for 15 minutes, then brush them with a little egg yolk and press the almonds on as shown in the picture. Bake the Santa Claus bread in a hot oven (220 C, 425 F, Gas 7) for 20 minutes then cool them on a wire rack.

For the icing, beat the egg white into the icing sugar. Place it in a small piping bag fitted with a plain nozzle and pipe the features on the cooled Santa Claus. Pipe small dots of icing to stick the sweets on the bread.

Kugelhopf

**Cooking temperature moderately hot
(200 C, 400 F, Gas 6)
and moderate (180 C, 350 F, Gas 4)
Cooking time 70–80 minutes**

225 g/8 oz strong plain flour
pinch of salt
25 g/1 oz fresh yeast or 3 teaspoons dried yeast
3 tablespoons lukewarm milk
75 g/3 oz butter
50 g/2 oz sugar
2 eggs
grated rind of $\frac{1}{2}$ lemon
pinch of nutmeg
2 tablespoons single cream
25 g/1 oz raisins
50 g/2 oz chopped candied peel
1 tablespoon rum
25 g/1 oz blanched almonds, roughly chopped
icing sugar to dust

Grease a Kugelhopf or fluted ring mould and dust it with a little flour. Sift the flour and salt into a bowl, making a hollow in the centre. Cream the yeast with a little of the milk, add the remaining milk and pour it into the middle of the flour. Sprinkle a little flour over the surface of the yeast liquid and leave it in a warm place for 15 minutes. Alternatively, if using dried yeast, pour the milk into the middle of the flour and sprinkle over the yeast. Stir it lightly into the milk, then leave it in a warm place until frothy.

Meanwhile, beat the butter with the sugar until creamy, then gradually add the eggs, grated lemon rind, nutmeg and the cream. Add this mixture to the yeast liquid and gradually beat in the flour until it is smooth and light. Mix the raisins and candied peel together, pour over the rum and leave the fruit to soak for a few minutes. Quickly mix the fruit into the batter with the almonds, taking care not to stir more than is necessary as the batter may turn slightly grey in colour.

Turn the batter into the prepared mould, cover it with cling film and let it rest in a warm place for 30 minutes. The batter should double in volume. Bake the Kugelhopf in a moderately hot oven (200 C, 400 F, Gas 6) for 40 minutes then reduce the temperature to moderate (180 C, 350 F, Gas 4) and cook it for a further 30–40 minutes.

Turn out and cool the Kugelhopf slightly on a wire rack, then dust it with icing sugar and serve warm.

Jam doughnuts

450 g / 1 lb strong plain flour
½ teaspoon salt
25 g / 1 oz fresh yeast or 3 teaspoons dried yeast
250 ml / 8 fl oz lukewarm milk
50 g / 2 oz butter
50 g / 2 oz caster sugar
2 egg yolks
grated rind of ½ lemon
3–4 tablespoons apricot or raspberry jam
oil for deep frying
icing sugar to dust

Sift the flour and salt into a bowl, making a hollow in the centre. Cream the yeast with a little of the milk, add the remaining milk and pour it into the middle of the flour. Sprinkle a little flour over the surface of the yeast liquid and leave it in a warm place for 15 minutes. Alternatively, if using dried yeast, pour the milk into the middle of the flour and sprinkle over the yeast. Stir it lightly into the milk, then leave it in a warm place until frothy.

Melt the butter and add it to the yeast liquid together with the sugar, egg yolks and lemon rind. Knead the dough well for 10 minutes until smooth. Place it in an oiled bowl, cover with cling film and leave it in a warm place for 40 minutes. Knead the risen dough lightly and divide it into 10 equal pieces. Knead each piece into a ball and make an indentation in the middle. Place a little of the jam in the hole and carefully pinch the dough around it to seal it in the middle. Place the doughnuts on a floured baking tray, cover them with oiled cling film and leave them in a warm place for 15–20 minutes until doubled in size. Heat the oil for deep frying to 180 C / 350 F and fry the doughnuts until golden brown, turning them over once during cooking to enable both sides to brown. Drain the doughnuts on absorbent kitchen paper and dust them with icing sugar when cold.

Alternatively, happy faces may be piped on the doughnuts using white icing (see Santa Claus bread, page 23).

Cream cheese crumble cake

Cooking temperature moderately hot
(200 C, 400 F, Gas 6)
Cooking time 30–40 minutes

350 g / 12 oz plain flour
20 g / ¾ oz fresh yeast
6 tablespoons lukewarm milk
50 g / 2 oz butter, melted
50 g / 2 oz caster sugar
2 eggs
pinch of salt
FILLING
175 g / 6 oz butter, softened
175 g / 6 oz caster sugar
3 eggs
575 g / 1¼ lb curd or cream cheese
25 g / 1 oz cornflour
grated rind of 1 lemon
100 g / 4 oz raisins (optional)
TOPPING
175 g / 6 oz plain flour
50 g / 2 oz sugar
pinch of salt
¼ teaspoon cinnamon
75 g / 3 oz butter

Sift the flour into a mixing bowl and make a well in the centre. Cream the yeast with the lukewarm milk and pour it into the well. Sprinkle the surface with a little of the flour. Cover and leave it in a warm place for 15 minutes, until frothy. Pour the melted butter into the flour together with the sugar, eggs and salt. Work all the ingredients together to make a dough. Knead lightly, cover and leave to rise in a warm place for 1 hour.

Beat the butter and sugar until light and creamy. Add the eggs, cheese, cornflour, lemon rind and raisins, if used.

Knead the dough and roll it out to line the base of a greased 23 × 33-cm / 9 × 13-in swiss roll tin. Spread the cheese mixture on top.

To make the crumble topping, mix together the flour, sugar, salt and cinnamon. Melt the butter and gradually add it to the flour, rubbing it in with the finger-tips. Sprinkle this mixture over the cheese filling and leave in a warm place for 15 minutes. Bake in a moderately hot oven (200 C, 400 F, Gas 6) for 30–40 minutes. Cool and cut into squares.

Cream cheese crumble cake

Danish pastries

(Illustrated on opposite page)

**Cooking temperature moderately hot
(200 C, 400 F, Gas 6)
and moderate (180 C, 350 F, Gas 4)
Cooking time 25 minutes**

450 g/1 lb strong plain flour
1 teaspoon salt
40 g/1½ oz fresh yeast or 4½ teaspoons dried
yeast
250 ml/8 fl oz lukewarm milk
50 g/2 oz butter, melted
50 g/2 oz caster sugar
175 g/6 oz butter, for rolling
50 g/2 oz plain flour
FILLING
100 g/4 oz hazelnuts, lightly toasted and ground
50 g/2 oz blanched almonds, lightly toasted and
ground
75 g/3 oz caster sugar
1 egg white
1 teaspoon cinnamon
ICING
100 g/4 oz icing sugar
juice of 1 lemon

Grease two baking trays. Sift the flour and salt into a bowl and make a hollow in the middle. Cream the yeast with a little of the lukewarm milk, add the remaining milk and pour it into the middle of the flour. Sprinkle a little flour over the surface of the yeast liquid and leave it in a warm place for 15 minutes. If using dried yeast, pour the milk into the flour, sprinkle over the yeast and stir lightly, then leave it in a warm place until frothy.

Mix the melted butter and sugar into the yeast liquid and gradually stir all the ingredients together to form a stiff dough. Knead the dough thoroughly for 10 minutes then place it in a lightly oiled bowl, cover with cling film and leave it to rest in the refrigerator for 15 minutes. Meanwhile, cream the butter and the flour for rolling and chill thoroughly. Shape it into a 15-cm/6-in square and again chill it thoroughly.

Roll out the dough to give an oblong measuring 20 × 38 cm/8 × 15 in and roughly mark it length-ways into thirds. Place the chilled block of butter on the middle third, fold the bottom third over it and fold the top third down to enclose it com-pletely. Press the edges together with a rolling pin and give the dough a quarter turn in a clockwise direction so that the folded edges are at the sides. Roll out the dough to the size of the original oblong, fold the pastry in thirds as before and chill, covered, for 30 minutes. Repeat this rolling, folding and chilling process twice more, then chill the dough for a further 30 minutes.

Cut the dough in half and roll one piece out to give an oblong measuring 20 × 30 cm/8 × 12 in. Make the filling by mixing the hazelnuts, almonds and sugar together with the egg white and cinna-mon to form a fairly soft paste, adding a little water if necessary. The pastries may be shaped in several ways. They may be made into combs or windmills following the directions for Iced puff pastries (page 42) or may be shaped in cartwheels or crescents.

To make cartwheels, cut the rolled out dough into four strips measuring 5 × 30 cm/2 × 12 in, spread half the filling along the strips and roll them up. For crescents, cut six long triangles measuring 10 cm/4 in at the wide end and 30 cm/ 12 in. in length to the pointed end. Spread half the filling over them and roll up from the wide end. Roll out the second piece of dough to a rectangle similar in size to the first and shape it as required.

Place the shaped pastries on the prepared baking trays and cover them with lightly greased cling film. Leave the pastries in a warm place for 30 minutes. Bake the risen Danish pastries in a moderately hot oven (200 C, 400 F, Gas 6) for 10 minutes, then reduce the temperature to moderate (180 C, 350 F, Gas 4) and cook them for a further 15 minutes. Cool the pastries on a wire rack.

Sift the icing sugar into a bowl and beat in the lemon juice to give a smooth, thin icing. Ice the cool pastries before serving them.

Suitable for freezing: The uncooked dough may be frozen when it is ready for shaping – pack and freeze it for up to 2 months. Allow the dough to defrost at room temperature before shaping the pastries.

Danish pastries

Plum slice

(Illustrated on page 10)

**Cooking temperature moderate
(180 C, 350 F, Gas 4)
Cooking time 40 minutes**

350 g/12 oz strong plain flour
½ teaspoon salt
15 g/½ oz fresh yeast or 1½ teaspoons dried yeast
150 ml/¼ pint lukewarm milk
100 g/4 oz butter
1 egg, lightly beaten
50 g/2 oz caster sugar
FILLING
1 kg/2 lb plums
50 g/2 oz caster sugar
½ teaspoon cinnamon

Lightly grease a 23 × 33-cm/9 × 13-in swiss roll tin. Sift the flour and salt into a bowl, making a hollow in the centre. Cream the yeast with a little of the milk, add the remaining milk and pour it into the middle of the flour. Sprinkle a little flour over the surface of the yeast liquid and leave it in a warm place for 15 minutes. Alternatively, if using dried yeast, pour the milk into the middle of the flour and sprinkle over the yeast. Stir it lightly into the milk, then leave it in a warm place until frothy.

Melt the butter, add the egg and sugar, then mix into the yeast liquid. Gradually stir in the flour to make a dough and knead it for 10 minutes until smooth. Place the dough in a lightly oiled bowl, cover with cling film and leave it to rise in a warm place for 30–40 minutes. Lightly knead and roll out the risen dough on a floured surface to an oblong large enough to line the prepared tin. Prick it all over with a fork. Halve and stone the plums and arrange them on the dough base, then sprinkle over the sugar and cinnamon. Leave the tin in a warm place for 15 minutes.

Bake the plum slice in a moderate oven (180 C, 350 F, Gas 4) for 40 minutes. Cut the cooked dough into serving portions and eat it warm or cold.

Sweet plum rounds

(Illustrated on opposite page)

**Cooking temperature moderately hot
(200 C, 400 F, Gas 6)
Cooking time 20–25 minutes**

450 g/1 lb plain flour
pinch of salt
25 g/1 oz fresh yeast
250 ml/8 fl oz lukewarm milk
75 g/3 oz caster sugar
50 g/2 oz butter, melted
grated rind of $\frac{1}{2}$ lemon
1 egg, beaten
1 egg yolk, beaten to glaze
FILLING
450 g/1 lb curd or cream cheese
50 g/2 oz butter, softened
200 g/7 oz caster sugar
2 eggs, separated
1 tablespoon cornflour
1 tablespoon rum
250 g/9 oz poppy seeds, ground
75 g/3 oz sugar
1 tablespoon fresh white breadcrumbs
250 ml/8 fl oz milk
250 g/9 oz stewed plums, puréed

Grease a baking tray. Sift the flour and salt into a bowl and make a well in the middle. Cream the yeast with a little of the milk, add the remaining milk and pour into the middle of the flour. Sprinkle a little of the flour over the surface of the liquid and leave it in a warm place for 15 minutes. Mix the sugar, melted butter, lemon rind and beaten egg into the flour with the yeast liquid. Knead the dough for 10 minutes and leave it in a warm place for 30 minutes. Lightly knead the risen dough before use.

To make the filling, beat the cheese with the butter, caster sugar and egg yolks. Whisk the whites until stiff and fold them into the mixture. Mix the cornflour and rum to a smooth cream.

Stir the poppy seeds, sugar, breadcrumbs and milk together and bring to the boil, then cool.

Divide the dough into 50-g/2-oz pieces. Shape them into rounds, pinching up the edges to form a rim, and place them on the prepared baking tray. Brush them with beaten egg yolk. Put 4 small spoonfuls of the cheese mixture and 4 small spoonfuls of the poppy mixture alternately into each round and a spoonful of the puréed plums in the centre. Cover and leave them to rise for 10 minutes. Bake in a moderately hot oven (200 C, 400 F, Gas 6) for 20–25 minutes.

Crisp butter squares

**Cooking temperature hot
(220 C, 425 F, Gas 7)
Cooking time 15–25 minutes**

450 g/1 lb strong plain flour
$\frac{1}{2}$ teaspoon salt
25 g/1 oz fresh yeast or 3 teaspoons dried yeast
250 ml/8 fl oz lukewarm milk
100 g/4 oz butter
50 g/2 oz caster sugar
1 egg, lightly beaten
grated rind of $\frac{1}{2}$ lemon
TOPPING
100 g/4 oz butter
150 g/5 oz blanched almonds, chopped
100 g/4 oz caster sugar
150 ml/$\frac{1}{4}$ pint soured cream

Grease two 23 × 33-cm/9 × 13-in swiss roll tins. Sift the flour and salt into a bowl, making a hollow in the centre. Cream the yeast with a little of the milk, add the remaining milk and pour it into the middle of the flour. Sprinkle a little flour over the surface of the yeast liquid and leave it in a warm place for 15 minutes. Alternatively, if using dried yeast, pour the milk into the middle of the flour and sprinkle over the yeast. Stir it lightly into the milk, then leave it in a warm place until frothy.

Melt the butter and add with the sugar, egg, and grated lemon rind to the yeast liquid, then stir in the dry ingredients to give a smooth dough. Knead this thoroughly for 10 minutes then place it in a lightly oiled bowl, cover with cling film and leave it in a warm place for 30–40 minutes. Lightly knead the risen dough and divide it in half. Roll each piece out to line one of the swiss roll tins and prick it all over with a fork. Dot the butter over the top and sprinkle with the chopped almonds and sugar. Spread the soured cream over the cakes and bake them in a hot oven (220 C, 425 F, Gas 7) until crisp and brown – about 15–25 minutes. Cool the cakes slightly in the tins, then cut them into squares and transfer to a wire rack to cool completely.

Brioches

**Cooking temperature hot
(220 C, 425 F, Gas 7)
Cooking time 15–20 minutes**

450 g/1 lb strong plain flour
½ teaspoon salt
40 g/1½ oz fresh yeast or 4½ teaspoons dried
yeast
250 ml/8 fl oz lukewarm milk
100 g/4 oz butter
50 g/2 oz caster sugar
2 eggs
grated rind of ½ lemon
egg yolk to glaze

Grease 20 small brioche or patty tins. Sift the flour and salt into a bowl, making a hollow in the centre. Cream the yeast with a little of the milk, add the remaining milk and pour it into the middle of the flour. Sprinkle a little flour over the surface of the yeast liquid and leave it in a warm place for 15 minutes. Alternatively, if using dried yeast, pour the milk into the middle of the flour and sprinkle over the yeast. Stir it lightly into the milk, then leave it in a warm place until frothy.

Melt the butter, add the sugar, eggs and lemon rind and stir into the yeast liquid, then gradually stir in the flour to make a dough. Knead the dough thoroughly for 10 minutes until smooth, then place it in a lightly oiled bowl, cover with cling film and leave it in a warm place for 30–40 minutes. Lightly knead the risen dough and divide two-thirds of it into 20 equal pieces.

Roll each piece into a ball and place them in the greased tins. Divide the remaining dough into 20 small pieces and roll each into a small ball. Make an indentation in the middle of each piece of dough in the tins and place a smaller piece of dough on top.

Cover the brioches lightly with oiled cling film and leave them in a warm place for 15 minutes. Brush them with a little egg yolk and bake the brioches in a hot oven (220 C, 425 F, Gas 7) for 15–20 minutes. Cool on a wire rack.

Below: Sweet plum rounds

Fruit tartlets

(Illustrated on opposite page)

**Cooking temperature moderately hot
(190 C, 375 F, Gas 5)
Cooking time 15 minutes**

350 g/12 oz plain flour
200 g/7 oz butter or margarine
100 g/4 oz caster sugar
1 egg yolk
2 tablespoons water
CREAM FILLING
100 g/4 oz caster sugar
grated rind and juice of 1 lemon
150 ml/$\frac{1}{4}$ pint white wine
3 egg yolks
15 g/$\frac{1}{2}$ oz gelatine
2 tablespoons hot water
300 ml/$\frac{1}{2}$ pint whipping cream
TOPPING
1 (425-g/15-oz) can sliced peaches or pineapple,
strawberries or pitted cherries, drained
150 ml/$\frac{1}{4}$ pint syrup from canned fruit
1 teaspoon gelatine
DECORATION (*optional*)
150 ml/$\frac{1}{4}$ pint double cream
1 tablespoon chopped pistachio nuts

Sift the flour into a bowl, add the butter, cut in small pieces, and rub it in lightly until the mixture resembles fine breadcrumbs. Stir in the sugar and mix the ingredients into a soft dough with the egg yolk and water. Chill the pastry for 30 minutes.

Roll out the pastry thinly and use it to line individual tartlet or flan tins. Prick the pastry cases all over with a fork and chill them for 15 minutes in the refrigerator before baking in a moderately hot oven (190 C, 375 F, Gas 5) for 12–15 minutes. Allow the tartlets to cool slightly in the tins then carefully turn them out on to a wire rack and cool completely.

To make the cream filling, whisk the sugar with the lemon rind and juice, white wine and egg yolks in a bowl over a pan of hot water until the yolks are cooked and the mixture is thickened slightly. Leave to cool. Dissolve the gelatine in 2 tablespoons of hot water in a basin over a saucepan of boiling water, then stir it into the custard and leave until the mixture begins to set. Whip the cream and fold it into the filling. Fill the tartlet cases with the cream, smooth the top and leave them to set in the refrigerator. Top the tarts with pieces of drained canned fruit or fresh soft fruit when in season.

Heat the syrup from the canned fruit, sprinkle over the gelatine and leave it in a basin over a pan of hot water until dissolved. Allow to cool and set lightly, then spoon a little of it over the top of the tartlets and leave them until completely set. Whip the double cream until stiff and place it in a piping bag fitted with a small star nozzle. Pipe decorative swirls of cream on the tartlets and sprinkle with chopped pistachio nuts before serving.

Cheese shapes

**Cooking temperature moderately hot
(200 C, 400 F, Gas 6)
Cooking time 10–15 minutes**

150 g/5 oz butter
175 g/6 oz Gruyère or Emmental cheese, grated
6 tablespoons single cream
$\frac{1}{2}$ teaspoon salt
1 teaspoon paprika
250 g/9 oz plain flour
$\frac{1}{2}$ teaspoon baking powder
1 egg yolk to glaze
TOPPING
poppy seeds, caraway seeds, coarse salt,
blanched almonds and chopped pistachio nuts

Lightly grease a baking tray. Beat the butter and the cheese together until pale and soft. Beat in the cream, salt and paprika. Sift the flour and baking powder together and work them into the creamed mixture to make a pastry dough. Allow the pastry to rest in the refrigerator for 2 hours.

Knead it lightly and roll out the pastry to 5 mm/$\frac{1}{4}$ in thick. Use biscuit cutters to cut the pastry out in various small shapes of your choice. Place these on the prepared baking tray and brush them with a little egg yolk. Sprinkle the top of the biscuits with a selection of any of the toppings and bake them in a moderately hot oven (200 C, 400 F, Gas 6) until lightly browned – about 10–15 minutes. The biscuits should not be over browned or they may become bitter.

Fruit tartlets

Cherry tarts

Cooking temperature moderately hot
(200 C, 400 F, Gas 6)
and moderate (180 C, 350 F, Gas 4)
Cooking time 30–35 minutes

125 g/4½ oz butter
90 g/3½ oz icing sugar
1 egg yolk
¼ teaspoon vanilla essence
pinch of salt
250 g/9 oz plain flour, sifted
FILLING
1 (425-g/15-oz) can pitted black cherries
150 ml/¼ pint double cream
6 tablespoons milk
50 g/2 oz butter
1 egg plus 1 egg yolk
15 g/½ oz cornflour
pinch of salt
2 teaspoons caster sugar

Cream the butter with the icing sugar until pale and soft. Beat in the egg yolk, vanilla essence and salt, then stir in the flour and knead lightly to form a pastry dough. Rest the dough in the refrigerator for an hour, then roll it out thinly and use it to line ten to twelve 7.5-cm/3-in flan tins. Prick the pastry cases all over with a fork and bake in a moderately hot oven (200 C, 400 F, Gas 6) for 10 minutes. Remove them from the oven and reduce the temperature to moderate (180 C, 350 F, Gas 4).
 Drain the cherries and divide them between the tartlets. Mix the remaining ingredients in a pan and heat gently until thickened, stirring continuously to prevent the sauce from burning. Spread this sauce over the cherries and bake the tarts for a further 20–25 minutes until lightly browned. Allow them to cool slightly in their tins, then transfer them to a wire rack to cool completely before serving.

Variation
Canned peaches, apricots or pears can be used instead of the cherries in this recipe. Alternatively, use prepared fresh fruit, for example stoned plums, sliced bananas or peeled, cored and sliced cooking apples.

Strawberry macaroon flan

Cooking temperature moderately hot
(200 C, 400 F, Gas 6)
Cooking time 25–30 minutes

150 g/5 oz butter
75 g/3 oz icing sugar
1 egg yolk
grated rind of ½ lemon
pinch of salt
225 g/8 oz plain flour, sifted
FILLING
50 g/2 oz butter
100 g/4 oz caster sugar
2 eggs
50 g/2 oz self-raising flour, sifted
225 g/8 oz ground almonds
DECORATION
350 g/12 oz strawberries
150 ml/¼ pint double cream
25 g/1 oz icing sugar

Cream the butter with the icing sugar until pale and soft. Stir in the egg yolk, lemon rind, salt and flour and knead together lightly to form a pastry dough. Leave the pastry to rest in the refrigerator for 30 minutes, then roll it out to line a 25-cm/10-in loose-bottomed flan tin. Prick the base all over with a fork and bake blind in a moderately hot oven (200 C, 400 F, Gas 6) for 15 minutes.
 To make the filling, cream the butter with the sugar until soft and creamy, then beat in the eggs and fold in the flour and ground almonds. Spread this mixture over the half-baked flan case and bake it for a further 25–30 minutes until golden brown, then leave it to cool. Meanwhile, hull and halve the strawberries. Whip the cream with the sugar until stiff and spoon it into a piping bag fitted with a star nozzle. Turn the cooled flan out on to a serving plate and pipe a border of cream around the edge. Fill the middle with the halved strawberries and dust the top with icing sugar before serving.

Alsatian apple flan

(Illustrated below)

**Cooking temperature moderately hot
(200 C, 400 F, Gas 6)
Cooking time 40–50 minutes**

200 g/7 oz plain flour
100 g/4 oz butter or margarine
1 egg yolk
25 g/1 oz caster sugar
pinch of salt
FILLING
450 g/1 lb small cooking apples
100 g/4 oz caster sugar
3 eggs
150 ml/¼ pint single cream

Sift the flour into a bowl, add the butter or margarine cut in small pieces and rub it in until the mixture resembles fine breadcrumbs. Add the egg yolk, sugar and salt and mix all the ingredients together to form a pastry dough. Rest the pastry in the refrigerator for 30 minutes, then roll it out and use it to line a 25-cm/10-in loose-bottomed flan tin. Prick the pastry all over with a fork.

Peel, core and halve the apples. Thinly slice the apple halves without separating the slices and arrange them on the pastry base. Bake the flan in a moderately hot oven (200 C, 400 F, Gas 6) for 20 minutes until the apples are lightly cooked. Beat the sugar with the eggs and cream and pour the mixture over the fruit.

Bake the flan for a further 20–30 minutes until the custard is set and lightly browned. Serve hot or cold.

Alsatian apple flan

Lemon flan

**Cooking temperature moderately hot
(190 C, 375 F, Gas 5)
Cooking time 30 minutes**

300 g/10 oz plain flour
200 g/7 oz butter
100 g/4 oz icing sugar
1 egg
grated rind of 1 lemon
FILLING
50 g/2 oz caster sugar
50 g/2 oz butter, melted
grated rind and juice of 2 lemons
2 eggs
15 g/½ oz gelatine
3 tablespoons hot water
DECORATION
75 g/3 oz sugar
4 tablespoons water
1 lemon, thinly sliced
7 glacé cherries

Lightly grease a 25-cm/10-in loose-bottomed flan tin. Sift the flour into a bowl and rub in the butter. Add the icing sugar, egg and lemon rind and mix together to make a smooth pastry dough. Chill the pastry for 2 hours. Roll out the dough quite thickly and use it to line the flan tin. Prick it all over with a fork and bake it blind in a moderately hot oven (190 C, 375 F, Gas 5) for 30 minutes.

Whisk the sugar, butter, lemon rind and juice with the eggs in a bowl over a saucepan of hot water until pale and creamy. Meanwhile, dissolve the gelatine in the hot water in a basin over a saucepan of hot water. Remove the egg mixture from the heat and continue whisking until it cools, then whisk in the dissolved gelatine and pour it into the cooled pastry case. Chill until set.

Dissolve the sugar for the decoration in the water over a low heat, then bring it to the boil and cook it for 5 minutes. Add the lemon slices and cook for 1–2 minutes, then carefully lift them out and arrange them on the flan together with the glacé cherries. Glaze the top with the remaining syrup and chill before serving.

Cheesecake

**Cooking temperature moderately hot
(200 C, 400 F, Gas 6)
Cooking time 50 minutes**

250 g/9 oz plain flour
150 g/5 oz butter
25 g/1 oz caster sugar
1 egg yolk
3–4 tablespoons water
FILLING
25 g/1 oz cornflour
100 g/4 oz sugar
450 ml/¾ pint milk
50 g/2 oz butter
few drops vanilla essence
grated rind of 1 lemon
225 g/8 oz cream cheese
3 eggs, separated
icing sugar to dust

Sift the flour into a bowl, rub in the butter and stir in the sugar and egg yolk together with enough water to give a shortcrust pastry. Knead the pastry lightly together and allow it to rest in the refrigerator for 1 hour. Roll out the pastry to line a 25-cm/10-in loose-bottomed flan tin and bake it blind for 15 minutes.

To make the filling, blend the cornflour with the sugar and a little of the milk until smooth. Heat the remaining milk and stir it into the cornflour, then return it to the pan and bring it to the boil. Remove the pan from the heat and stir in the butter, vanilla essence and lemon rind. Finally, beat in the cream cheese and egg yolks and allow the mixture to cool.

Whisk the egg whites until stiff and fold into the cooled mixture. Turn the cheese mixture into the flan case and bake it for a further 25–35 minutes until lightly browned and set. Cool completely. Before serving, dust the top of the cheesecake with icing sugar.

Cheese puffs (page 41)

Beef pasties

Cooking temperature moderately hot
(200 C, 400 F, Gas 6)
Cooking time 25–30 minutes

1 (368-g/13-oz) packet frozen puff pastry,
thawed
450 g/1 lb minced beef
1 small onion, finely chopped
1 clove garlic, crushed
$\frac{1}{2}$ teaspoon salt
dash of Tabasco sauce
$\frac{1}{2}$ teaspoon dried marjoram
2 egg yolks

Moisten a baking tray with a little water. Roll the pastry out into a 40-cm/16-in square and cut out 16 10-cm/4-in squares. Mix the beef with the onion, garlic, salt, Tabasco, marjoram and one of the egg yolks. Divide the mixture between the squares and brush the edges with a little of the remaining egg yolk mixed with 1 tablespoon water. Press the edges together well to seal the filling in the middle. Roll the pasties to shape them evenly and use any pastry trimmings to decorate them. Place the pasties on the prepared baking tray and brush the tops with the remaining egg yolk. Bake them in a moderately hot oven (200 C, 400 F, Gas 6) for about 25–30 minutes.

Ham and cheese horns

Cooking temperature moderately hot
(200 C, 400 F, Gas 6)
Cooking time 25 minutes

1 (368-g/13-oz) packet frozen puff pastry,
thawed
1 egg, beaten to glaze
FILLING
75 g/3 oz Gouda cheese
100 g/4 oz cooked ham
1 egg yolk
1 tablespoon each chopped onion and parsley
pinch each of pepper and dried oregano

Dampen the two baking trays. On a floured board, roll out the pastry into a sheet measuring 58 × 25 cm/23 × 10 in. Cut into 15 triangles, each with two very long sides (see illustration).

Finely dice the cheese and ham and mix with the egg yolk, parsley, onion, pepper and oregano. Place about 2 teaspoons of the filling towards the bottom of each triangle. Make a small cut in the short side of the triangle (see illustration) and roll the triangles loosely into horn shapes.

Place the horns on the prepared baking trays. Brush with beaten egg and leave them in the refrigerator for 15 minutes. Preheat the oven to moderately hot (200 C, 400 F, Gas 6) and bake the horns towards the top of the oven for 25 minutes.

Caraway and poppy-seed rings

Cooking temperature hot
(220 C, 425 F, Gas 7)
Cooking time 8–10 minutes

1 (368-g/13-oz) packet frozen puff pastry,
thawed
1 egg yolk
50 g/2 oz Emmental or Gruyère cheese, finely
grated
TOPPING
2 tablespoons poppy seeds
2 tablespoons caraway seeds

Moisten a baking tray with a little water. Roll out the pastry to 5 mm/$\frac{1}{4}$ in thick. Brush with a little of the egg yolk and sprinkle the cheese over half the pastry. Fold over the other half and press down well. Roll out again to about 3 mm/$\frac{1}{8}$ in thick.

Use a biscuit cutter to cut out 5-cm/2-in circles. Cut out a 1-cm/$\frac{1}{2}$-in round from the middle of each biscuit and place these rings on the prepared baking tray. Add 1 tablespoon of water to the remaining egg yolk and brush it over them. Sprinkle the biscuits with either poppy or caraway seeds and chill them for 10–15 minutes before baking them in a hot oven (220 C, 425 F, Gas 7) until lightly browned – about 8–10 minutes. Cool on a wire rack.

Clockwise from the top: Caraway and poppy-seed rings, Ham and cheese horns, baked and in preparation, and Beef pasties

Caraway cheese sticks

(Illustrated on opposite page)

**Cooking temperature hot
(220 C, 425 F, Gas 7)
Cooking time 7–10 minutes**

1 (368-g/13-oz) packet frozen puff pastry,
thawed
1 egg yolk to glaze
FILLING
75 g/3 oz Emmental or Gruyère cheese,
finely grated
1 teaspoon paprika
freshly ground pepper
TOPPING
caraway seeds

Moisten a baking tray with a little water. Roll the pastry out into a sheet measuring 20 × 40 cm/ 8 × 16 in. Brush the puff pastry with a little of the egg yolk and sprinkle the cheese, paprika and pepper evenly over one half of it. Fold the other half over and press down well. Roll out to an oblong similar in size to the original sheet and cut off 1-cm/½-in wide strips measuring 20 cm/8 in in length. Twist the strips into spirals, place them on the prepared baking tray and brush with the remaining egg yolk. Sprinkle with the caraway seeds and bake in a hot oven (220 C, 425 F, Gas 7) for 7–10 minutes. They should not be too brown, but golden. Cool on a wire rack.

Fleurons

**Cooking temperature hot
(220 C, 425 F, Gas 7)
Cooking time 5–10 minutes**

1 (368-g/13-oz) packet frozen puff pastry,
thawed
egg yolk to glaze

Moisten a baking tray with a little water. Roll out the pastry evenly to 3–5 mm/⅛–¼ in thick. Use a 3.5-cm/1½-in fluted pastry cutter to cut out first circles, then half-moon shapes and place them on the prepared baking tray. The top of the pastry may be lightly scored in a decorative criss-cross design. To do this, use a sharp pointed knife and cut the pastry before glazing it. Stir the egg yolk with 2 tablespoons water, brush the fleurons with this mixture and bake in a hot oven (220 C, 425 F, Gas 7) until well puffed and golden – about 5–10 minutes.

Orange twists

**Cooking temperature hot
(220 C, 425 F, Gas 7)
Cooking time 15 minutes**

1 (368-g/13-oz) packet frozen puff pastry,
thawed
FILLING
50 g/2 oz chopped candied peel
175 g/6 oz ground almonds
50 g/2 oz icing sugar
grated rind and juice of 1 orange
1 tablespoon rum
2 egg yolks
egg yolk to glaze
50 g/2 oz blanched almonds, chopped

Grease a baking tray. Roll the pastry out into a sheet measuring approximately 30 × 40 cm/ 12 × 16 in. To make the filling, mix the chopped peel with the ground almonds, icing sugar and orange rind and juice. Stir in the rum and egg yolks. Spread this filling over half the pastry and fold over the other half, pressing it down well to give an oblong measuring 15 × 20 cm/6 × 8 in. Cut into eight 15-cm/6-in strips, each measuring 2.5 cm/1 in. in width. Twist the strips once and place them on the prepared baking tray. Brush each with a little egg yolk, sprinkle them with the chopped almonds and bake in a hot oven (220 C, 425 F, Gas 7) for 15 minutes until golden brown and well puffed. Cool on a wire rack.

Top: Caraway cheese sticks
and Gouda pearls (page 46);
Bottom: Layered cheese puff (page 41)

Cheese puffs

(Illustrated on page 35)

Cooking temperature hot
(220 C, 425 F, Gas 7)
Cooking time 8–10 minutes

1 (368-g/13-oz) packet frozen puff pastry,
thawed
75 g/3 oz Gruyère cheese, grated
2 tablespoons milk
1 egg yolk
75 g/3 oz Emmental cheese, grated
$\frac{1}{2}$ teaspoon paprika

Dampen a baking tray and cut the pastry in half.
To make cheese bows, sprinkle some of the Gruyère cheese over the pastry board or work surface and roll out one piece of the puff pastry on it, to a thickness of 5 mm/$\frac{1}{4}$ in. Whisk together the milk and egg yolk and use to glaze the surface of the pastry. Sprinkle with more of the Gruyère cheese, fold the pastry up and roll it out again. Sprinkle the rest of the cheese over the surface, fold up and finally roll the pastry out to 3 mm/$\frac{1}{8}$ in thick. Cut into 7.5-cm/3-in strips and lay them four strips at a time on top of one another. Cut 5-mm/$\frac{1}{4}$-in wide slices from these and twist to form bows.
Arrange the bows on the prepared baking tray and leave to rest for 15 minutes. Bake the cheese bows in a hot oven (220 C, 425 F, Gas 7) for 8–10 minutes.
Repeat the same process with the second half of the pastry, but this time sprinkle the pastry with the grated Emmental and paprika mixed together. Cut into 10-cm/4-in long narrow strips. Brush these with the rest of the egg yolk glaze and sprinkle with the rest of the cheese. Bake these cheese straws as above.

Variation

Delicious canapés can be made with this cheese pastry. Roll the pastry as above and cut out small oval shapes. Bake as above and cool on a wire rack. Sandwich pairs of these together with beaten and piped cream cheese, softened with a little cream. Sprinkle with poppy seeds or caraway seeds and garnish as illustrated in the picture.

Layered cheese puff

(Illustrated on page 38)

Cooking temperature hot
(220 C, 425 F, Gas 7)
Cooking time 10–12 minutes

2 (368-g/13-oz) packets frozen puff pastry,
thawed
FILLING
450 g/1 lb cream cheese
2 egg yolks
salt and pepper
pinch of caster sugar
150 ml/$\frac{1}{4}$ pint double cream
2 teaspoons paprika
2 tablespoons chopped mixed fresh herbs
GARNISH
2 stuffed olives
4 cocktail onions
4 small chillies
1–2 teaspoons chopped pistachio nuts

Moisten three baking trays with a little water. Press both pieces of puff pastry together well and roll out into a sheet large enough to cut out three 20-cm/8-in circles. Place these on the prepared baking trays and prick them all over with a fork. Rest the pastry in the refrigerator for 10–15 minutes, then bake it in a hot oven (220 C, 425 F, Gas 7) until well puffed and golden – about 10–12 minutes. Cool on a wire rack.
Beat the cream cheese with the egg yolks, seasoning and the sugar until creamy. Whip the cream until stiff and fold it into the cheese mixture. Divide this mixture into three equal portions. Stir the paprika into one portion and spread this over one round of pastry. Mix the herbs into a second portion and spread it over another piece of pastry. Place this on top of the paprika cream and top with the third round of pastry.
Place the remaining, unflavoured cheese mixture in a piping bag fitted with a star nozzle and pipe decorative twists of cream on top of the pastry. Decorate with halved olives, cocktail onions and chillies. Sprinkle with the pistachio nuts and serve it cut into small portions with drinks or with a crisp salad for a light lunch.

Iced puff pastries (page 42)

Iced puff pastries

(Illustrated on page 40)

Cooking temperature hot
(220 C, 425 F, Gas 7)
Cooking time 10–15 minutes

1 (368-g/13-oz) packet frozen puff pastry,
thawed
FILLING
75 g/3 oz hazelnuts, ground
40 g/1½ oz caster sugar
1 tablespoon rum
1 egg, separated
6 canned apricot halves, drained
ICING
100 g/4 oz apricot jam
75 g/3 oz icing sugar
2–3 tablespoons water

Dampen two baking trays. Roll out the pastry and trim it to give an oblong measuring 30 × 40 cm/ 12 × 16 in. Cut out twelve 10-cm/4-in squares.

To make the filling, mix the hazelnuts with the sugar, rum and enough of the egg white to bind the mixture together. Spread the nut mixture thinly over the middle of half the pastry squares. Place an apricot half in the middle of each of the remaining pastry squares and lightly brush the edges of all the squares with a little of the egg yolk.

Fold the nut-filled pastry squares in half, pressing the pastry together well, then cut in towards the folded end to achieve a comb effect. Make four cuts inwards from the corners as far as the apricots on the remaining pastry squares and fold alternate corners over the apricots to make windmill shapes. Roll out the pastry trimmings and cut out six 1-cm/½-in squares, brush them with a little egg yolk and press them down on the top of each apricot to form the middle of the windmill. Place the pastries on the prepared baking trays and brush them lightly with a little egg yolk. Bake them in a hot oven (220 C, 425 F, Gas 7) for 10–15 minutes until well puffed and golden brown. Cool on a wire rack.

Warm and sieve the apricot jam and brush it lightly over the pastries. Sift the icing sugar into a bowl, then gradually beat in the water to make a smooth, thin icing. Spread the icing thinly over the apricot jam and leave it to set. These pastries are best eaten on the same day as baking.

Cream slices

Cooking temperature hot
(220 C, 425 F, Gas 7)
Cooking time 12–15 minutes

1 (368-g/13-oz) packet frozen puff pastry,
thawed
FILLING
40 g/1½ oz cornflour
600 ml/1 pint milk
1 vanilla pod, split
75 g/3 oz sugar
4 egg yolks
ICING
100 g/4 oz apricot jam
1–2 tablespoons water
1–2 tablespoons lemon juice
225 g/8 oz icing sugar, sifted

Dampen a baking tray. Roll out the pastry very thinly to the size of a 23 × 33-cm/9 × 13-in baking tray and place the pastry on the prepared tray. Prick it all over with a fork, cut it in half lengthways and leave to chill for 15 minutes in the refrigerator. Bake in a hot oven (220 C, 425 F, Gas 7) for 12–15 minutes until pale golden, then cool on a wire rack.

Mix the cornflour with a little of the milk to form a smooth cream. Heat the remaining milk with the vanilla pod and leave to infuse for 10 minutes before removing the pod. Stir the milk into the cornflour mixture then return it to the pan together with the sugar and bring it to the boil, stirring continuously to prevent lumps from forming. Remove from the heat and cool slightly, then stir in the egg yolks and cook gently for a few minutes without boiling. Cool the custard, stirring continuously, until just warm and thickened enough to spread over the pastry. Spread it over one piece of pastry and lay the second piece on top.

Warm and sieve the jam and brush it over the top of the pastry. Beat the water and lemon juice into the icing sugar and spread it over the jam. Leave until set, then use a very sharp knife to cut it into slices.

Swiss apricot tart

(Illustrated below)

Cooking temperature hot
(220 C, 425 F, Gas 7)
and moderately hot (200 C, 400 F, Gas 6)
Cooking time 25–30 minutes

1 (368-g/13-oz) packet frozen puff pastry,
thawed
FILLING
450 g/1 lb apricots
2 tablespoons fresh white breadcrumbs
3 eggs
250 ml/8 fl oz soured cream
75 g/3 oz caster sugar
grated rind of $\frac{1}{2}$ lemon

Roll out the puff pastry and use to line a 25-cm/
10-in loose-bottomed flan tin. Prick the pastry all
over with a fork and chill it for 30 minutes. Bake
the flan case in a hot oven (220 C, 425 F, Gas 7) for
8–10 minutes, then reduce the oven temperature
to moderately hot (200 C, 400 F, Gas 6).

Meanwhile, halve and stone the apricots.
Sprinkle the breadcrumbs over the pastry base
and arrange the apricot halves on top. Beat the
eggs with the soured cream, sugar and lemon rind
and pour this over the apricots. Bake for a further
25–30 minutes until golden brown and set. Serve
hot or cold.

Variation

For a quick alternative to this recipe use canned
fruit instead of the fresh apricots. Drain canned
apricots, peaches or plums and arrange them on
the pastry base as above. Grated orange rind may
be substituted for the lemon rind.

Swiss apricot tart

Cherry cream layer gâteau

(Illustrated below)

**Cooking temperature moderately hot
(200 C, 400 F, Gas 6)
Cooking time 10–12 minutes**

---

1 (368-g/13-oz) packet frozen puff pastry,
thawed
FILLING AND TOPPING
50 g/2 oz redcurrant jelly
100 g/4 oz icing sugar
1 tablespoon lemon juice
1 (425-g/15-oz) can red cherries
pinch of cinnamon
1 tablespoon cornflour
450 ml/$\frac{3}{4}$ pint double cream
40 g/$1\frac{1}{2}$ oz caster sugar
12 glacé cherries

Sprinkle three baking trays with a little cold water. Divide the pastry into three portions and roll out each into a 20-cm/8-in round. Place these on the baking trays and leave for 15 minutes. Bake in a moderately hot oven (200 C, 400 F, Gas 6) for 10–12 minutes, until lightly browned.

Cover the best pastry round with the warmed redcurrant jelly. Mix the sifted icing sugar and lemon juice together and spread this glaze over the jam. Leave to cool, then cut the glazed pastry layer into 12 slices.

Drain the cherries, reserving the juice. Heat the juice from the cherries with the cinnamon. Blend the cornflour with a little cold water and add to the cherry juice. Bring to the boil, stirring continuously, until slightly thickened. Stir in the stoned cherries and leave to cool. Spread the cooled cherry sauce over the bottom pastry layer.

Whip the cream with the caster sugar until stiff. Put about 5 tablespoons of this cream into a piping bag fitted with a star nozzle. Spread some of the remaining cream over the cherries and put the last uncovered pastry layer on top. Spread the remaining cream thickly over this and around the sides of the gateau. Arrange the glazed pastry slices on top and decorate each with a rosette of cream and a glacé cherry.

Cherry cream layer gâteau

Savoury choux puffs

(Illustrated below)

Cooking temperature hot
(220 C, 425 F, Gas 7)
Cooking time 20 minutes

CHOUX PASTRY
250 ml/8 fl oz water
50 g/2 oz butter
pinch of salt
200 g/7 oz plain flour, sifted
4 eggs
FILLING
100 g/4 oz cream cheese
$\frac{1}{2}$ teaspoon paprika
1 tablespoon chopped chives
3–4 tablespoons milk
GARNISH
stuffed olives, gherkins, walnut halves, glacé
cherries and red pepper strips

Grease a baking tray. Put the water in a small pan with the butter and a pinch of salt. Heat gently to melt the butter, then bring to the boil. Remove the pan from the heat and add the flour all at once. Mix with a wooden spoon to form a paste which leaves the sides of the pan clean. Cool, then beat in the eggs one at a time. Pipe or spoon the mixture in small puffs on to the prepared baking tray. Cook for about 20 minutes, until well risen and golden brown.

Remove them from the baking tray, cut in half and leave to cool on a wire rack. Mix the ingredients together for the filling and pipe some into the halved cheese puffs. Top with a swirl of the remaining filling. Garnish as illustrated.

Suitable for freezing: The cooled, unfilled choux buns may be frozen for up to 3 months. Allow the buns to defrost at room temperature then put them in a hot oven for about a minute before filling them.

Savoury choux puffs

Gouda pearls

(Illustrated on page 38)

Cooking temperature hot
(220 C, 425 F, Gas 7)
Cooking time 8–10 minutes

½ quantity choux pastry (Savoury choux puffs
page 45)
50 g/2 oz Gouda cheese, finely grated

Lightly grease a baking tray. Make the choux
pastry according to the recipe instructions, then
beat in the cheese. Spoon the pastry into a piping
bag fitted with a plain nozzle and pipe small buns
on to the prepared baking tray. Bake in a hot oven
(220 C, 425 F, Gas 7) for 8–10 minutes until well
puffed and golden. Make a small slit in the buns
immediately they are removed from the oven and
cool them on a wire rack. Alternatively, serve the
buns hot.

Variation

Add 2 tablespoons chopped fresh herbs, for
example thyme, parsley, sage and lemon balm,
to the choux pastry together with the cheese.
These hot buns are delicious with soup or as a
garnish for meat casseroles.

Raspberry puffs

(Illustrated below)

Cooking temperature hot
(220 C, 425 F, Gas 7)
and moderately hot (190 C, 375 F, Gas 5)
Cooking time 30–35 minutes

½ quantity choux pastry (Savoury choux puffs
page 45)
FILLING
300 ml/½ pint double cream
50 g/2 oz icing sugar
2 tablespoons cherry brandy (optional)
350 g/12 oz raspberries
icing sugar to dust

Lightly grease a baking tray. Make the choux
pastry according to the recipe instructions. Fit a
large star nozzle in a piping bag and fill it with the
choux pastry. Pipe 12 swirls of choux pastry on
the prepared baking tray and cook in a hot oven
(220 C, 425 F, Gas 7) for 10 minutes. Reduce the
temperature to moderately hot (190 C, 375 F, Gas 5)
and cook for a further 20–25 minutes. Remove
the buns to a wire rack and split them in half
immediately.
  Whip the cream with the sugar and cherry
brandy (if used) until stiff, then fold in the raspberries. Fill the cold puffs with the raspberry
cream and dust them with a little icing sugar before
serving.

Raspberry puffs

Cream-filled choux puffs

**Cooking temperature hot
(220 C, 425 F, Gas 7)
Cooking time 20 minutes**

250 ml/8 fl oz water
50 g/2 oz butter or margarine
pinch of salt
grated rind of ½ lemon
200 g/7 oz plain flour
4 eggs, beaten
FILLING
450 ml/¾ pint double cream
50 g/2 oz caster sugar
icing sugar to sprinkle

In a heavy-based pan gently heat the water with the butter or margarine, salt and lemon rind, until the fat is melted. Bring to the boil then tip in the sifted flour all at once, remove from the heat and beat well until the ingredients form a ball and come away from the sides of the pan. Return to the heat and cook for 1 minute, stirring all the time. Turn the mixture into a bowl, allow to cool slightly then add the eggs, a little at a time, beating well with each addition.

Pipe the choux paste in different shapes on to a baking tray, leaving sufficient space between each to allow for rising during cooking. Bake in a hot oven (220 C, 425 F, Gas 7) for 20 minutes. Do not open the oven door during the first 10 minutes' baking time, or the pastry will collapse.

While the choux puffs are still hot, split through them to let any steam escape. Allow to cool. Whip the cream stiffly with the sugar and pipe into each puff. Dust the tops with icing sugar.

Variation

You can pipe long éclair shapes from the choux paste and cook them as above. Fill these with coffee cream and ice them with a coffee icing.

Below: Flaky choux gâteau (page 48)

Gâteau Saint-Honoré

**Cooking temperature hot
(220 C, 425 F, Gas 7)
and moderately hot (190 C, 375 F, Gas 5)
Cooking time 30–35 minutes**

175 g/6 oz plain flour
pinch of salt
75 g/3 oz butter
40 g/1½ oz caster sugar
1 egg yolk
1 quantity choux pastry (Savoury choux puffs
page 45)
CUSTARD
25 g/1 oz cornflour
450 ml/¾ pint milk
100 g/4 oz caster sugar
½ teaspoon vanilla essence
4 egg yolks
icing sugar to dust

Grease a baking tray. Sift the flour and salt into a bowl, add the butter and rub it into the flour until the mixture resembles fine breadcrumbs. Stir in the sugar and egg yolk and mix the ingredients together to form a smooth pastry. Leave it to rest in the refrigerator for 30 minutes. Roll the chilled pastry out into a circle measuring 30 cm/12 in in diameter and lift it carefully on to the baking tray. Prick it all over with a fork.

Make the choux pastry according to the recipe instructions and place it in a piping bag fitted with a large star nozzle. Pipe a thick border of choux pastry around the edge of the pastry circle and use the remaining choux pastry to pipe small buns on the baking tray. Bake in a hot oven (220 C, 425 F, Gas 7) for 10 minutes, then reduce the temperature to moderately hot (190 C, 375 F, Gas 5) and cook for a further 20–25 minutes until the border is well puffed, golden brown and crisp.

To make the custard, cream the cornflour with a little of the milk, sugar and vanilla essence until smooth. Heat the remaining milk, stir it into the cornflour mixture then return to the pan and bring to the boil, stirring continuously to prevent it from burning. Remove the pan from the heat, allow it to cool slightly then stir in the egg yolks and cook for a few minutes without boiling. Cool until just warm, stirring frequently to prevent a skin from forming, then pour the custard into the pastry case and leave it until set. Sift a little icing sugar over the puffs and arrange them on top of the gâteau.

Flaky choux gâteau

(Illustrated on page 47)

**Cooking temperature hot
(220 C, 425 F, Gas 7)
and moderately hot (190 C, 375 F, Gas 5)
Cooking time 30–35 minutes**

½ quantity choux pastry (Savoury choux puffs
page 45)
FILLING
300 ml/½ pint double cream
100 g/4 oz icing sugar, sifted
few drops vanilla essence
grated rind of ½ lemon
2 egg whites
350 g/12 oz raspberries
icing sugar to dust

Lightly grease two baking trays. Make the choux pastry according to the recipe instructions.

Spread the mixture in two 18-cm/7-in rounds on the prepared baking trays and bake them in a hot oven (220 C, 425 F, Gas 7) for 10 minutes, then reduce the oven temperature to moderately hot (190 C, 375 F, Gas 5) and cook for a further 20–25 minutes until they are well puffed, crisp and golden brown. Cool on a wire rack.

Whip the cream with the icing sugar, vanilla essence and lemon rind until stiff. Whisk the egg whites until stiff and fold them into the cream. Split the choux rounds horizontally through the middle. Place one of the bases on a serving dish and spread a layer of cream over it. Reserve a few raspberries for decoration and arrange half the remainder on the cream. Top with the second choux pastry base and another layer of the cream followed by the remaining raspberries. Chop the last two pieces of choux pastry into small pieces. Spread the sides of the gâteau thinly with a little of the remaining cream, then cover the top and sides completely with the pieces of choux pastry. Sift a little icing sugar over the top and spoon the remaining cream into a piping bag fitted with a star nozzle. Pipe swirls of cream around the edge of the gâteau and decorate with the reserved raspberries.

Banana macaroons

Cooking temperature moderately hot
(190 C, 375 F, Gas 5)
Cooking time 15 minutes

MACAROONS
175 g/6 oz ground almonds
2 teaspoons ground rice
grated rind of $\frac{1}{2}$ lemon
175 g/6 oz caster sugar
3 egg whites
6 bananas, halved
CREAM
2 tablespoons vanilla flavoured blancmange
powder
500 ml/17 fl oz milk
2 egg yolks
175 g/6 oz caster sugar
225 g/8 oz butter, softened
2 tablespoons rum
ICING
225 g/8 oz plain chocolate
1 tablespoon chopped pistachio nuts

Grease a non-stick baking tray. Mix the ground almonds with the ground rice, lemon rind and sugar. Lightly whisk the egg whites and stir in the dry ingredients to give a smooth mixture. Fit a piping bag with a 1-cm/$\frac{1}{2}$-in plain nozzle and fill it with the mixture. Pipe 12 crescents, the same size and shape as the bananas, slightly apart on the greased baking tray. Bake these macaroons in a moderately hot oven (190 C, 375 F, Gas 5) for 15 minutes, then allow them to cool before removing them from the tray.

Blend the blancmange powder with the milk, egg yolks and sugar. Bring the mixture slowly to the boil, stirring continuously, then cover and leave it to cool. Gradually beat the butter and rum into the custard. Chill this cream before using it.

Fit a piping bag with a star nozzle, fill it with the cream and pipe some on each macaroon. Top with half a banana. Melt the chocolate in a basin over a saucepan of hot water and use to coat the macaroons, then sprinkle with pistachio nuts.

Banana macaroons

49

Frangipane cakes

(Illustrated below)

Cooking temperature moderately hot
(200 C, 400 F, Gas 6)
Cooking time 20–25 minutes

1 (368-g/13-oz) packet frozen puff pastry,
thawed
FILLING
75 g/3 oz apricot jam
100 g/4 oz butter or margarine
100 g/4 oz caster sugar
100 g/4 oz ground almonds
2 eggs
100 g/4 oz self-raising flour
½ teaspoon baking powder

Roll the pastry out thinly and cut out rounds to line 24 small brioche or patty tins. Prick the pastry cases with a fork to avoid bubbles forming during baking and spoon a little of the jam into each one.
　Beat the butter with the sugar until pale and creamy, then beat in the ground almonds and eggs. Sift the flour and baking powder together and fold into the mixture, then divide it between the pastry cases and smooth the tops. Bake in a moderately hot oven (200 C, 400 F, Gas 6) for 20–25 minutes until the cakes are well risen and golden brown. Cool on a wire rack.

Variation

Substitute your favourite jam for the apricot jam and beat the grated rind of a halved lemon or orange into the creamed mixture. Sift a little icing sugar over the cooked cakes before serving.

Frangipane cakes

Chocolate mallow biscuits

(Illustrated below)

**Cooking temperature moderately hot
(190 C, 375 F, Gas 5)
Cooking time 15 minutes**

---

150 g/5 oz butter
40 g/1½ oz icing sugar
2 egg yolks
200 g/7 oz plain flour
FILLING
4 tablespoons raspberry jam
225 g/8 oz marshmallows
100 g/4 oz plain chocolate
2 teaspoons rum
ICING
225 g/8 oz plain chocolate
50 g/2 oz hazelnuts, blanched

Lightly grease a baking tray. Beat the butter with the icing sugar and egg yolks until pale and soft.

Sift the flour over the creamed mixture and stir it in to make a dough. Knead lightly, then leave it to rest in the refrigerator for 1–2 hours.

Roll the pastry out to 3 mm/⅛ in thick and, using a biscuit cutter, cut out 3.5-cm/1½-in circles. Place them on the prepared baking tray and bake the biscuits in a moderately hot oven (190 C, 375 F, Gas 5) until lightly browned. Cool slightly on the trays then remove them to a wire rack to cool completely. Sandwich the biscuits together in pairs with the jam.

Melt the marshmallows and chocolate together in a basin over a saucepan of hot water, stirring to combine the ingredients. Stir in the rum and allow to cool. Fit a piping bag with a large star nozzle and spoon the mixture into it. Pipe the marshmallow topping into peaks on each biscuit sandwich. Chill for 2 hours to set the mixture completely. Melt the remaining chocolate in a basin over a saucepan of hot water and spoon it over the biscuits to coat them completely. Top each with a hazelnut and allow them to set before serving.

Chocolate mallow biscuits

Chocolate macaroon creams

Cooking temperature very cool
(110 C, 225 F, Gas ¼)
Cooking time 3–4 hours

5 egg whites
250 g/10 oz caster sugar
25 g/1 oz cornflour
175 g/6 oz ground almonds
FILLING
350 g/12 oz plain chocolate
1 egg yolk
50 g/2 oz caster sugar
2 tablespoons rum
150 ml/¼ pint double cream

Lightly grease a non-stick baking tray and dust it with a little flour. Whisk the egg whites until stiff then gradually whisk in the sugar until very stiff and glossy. Mix the cornflour with the ground almonds and carefully fold into the egg mixture. Spoon this mixture into a piping bag fitted with a large star nozzle and pipe even-sized swirls on the prepared baking tray. Dry out the macaroons in a very cool oven (110 C, 225 F, Gas ¼) for 3–4 hours, leaving the oven door slightly ajar if possible as this will allow any steam to escape.

Melt the chocolate in a basin over a saucepan of hot water. Whisk the egg yolk with the sugar until pale and creamy, then stir in the rum. Gradually stir the yolk mixture into the melted chocolate. Lightly whip the cream until it stands in soft peaks, then fold it into the chocolate mixture. Sandwich the macaroons together with the chocolate cream.

Almond kisses

Almond kisses

(Illustrated on opposite page)

225 g/8 oz slivered almonds
100 g/4 oz chopped candied peel
100 g/4 oz raisins
350 g/12 oz plain chocolate

Spread the almonds on a baking tray and toast them under a hot grill until lightly browned. Allow them to cool, then mix them with the candied peel and raisins. Melt the chocolate in a basin over a saucepan of hot water and stir it into the almond mixture. Spoon small heaps of the mixture into paper cake cases and allow the biscuits to set.

Garland biscuits

(Illustrated on the front cover and page 55)

Cooking temperature moderately hot
(200 C, 400 F, Gas 6)
Cooking time 10–15 minutes

4 hard-boiled egg yolks, sieved
75 g/3 oz icing sugar
200 g/7 oz butter
few drops of vanilla essence
275 g/10 oz plain flour
pinch of salt
egg yolk to glaze
100 g/4 oz blanched almonds, chopped
100 g/4 oz preserving or granulated sugar
100 g/4 oz raspberry jam

Grease a baking tray. Beat the egg yolks, icing sugar, butter and vanilla together until pale and soft. Sift the flour and salt together, stir into the mixture and knead it lightly. Allow the pastry to rest in the refrigerator for an hour, then roll it out to 3 mm/$\frac{1}{8}$ in thick and use a 5-cm/2-in biscuit cutter to cut out the biscuits.

Cut a 1-cm/$\frac{1}{2}$-in circle out of the middle and brush each with a little egg yolk. Place the biscuits on the baking tray and sprinkle the almonds and preserving or granulated sugar over them. Cook in a moderately hot oven (200 C, 400 F, Gas 6) until golden. Cool the biscuits on a wire rack, then sandwich them together in pairs with the jam.

Viennese vanilla crescents

(Illustrated on page 55)

Cooking temperature moderately hot
(190 C, 375 F, Gas 5)
Cooking time 10 minutes

50 g/2 oz blanched almonds
50 g/2 oz hazelnuts
275 g/10 oz plain flour
65 g/2$\frac{1}{2}$ oz caster sugar
pinch of salt
200 g/7 oz butter, cut into flakes
2 egg yolks
75 g/3 oz vanilla sugar
25 g/1 oz icing sugar

Grease a baking tray. Finely grate the almonds and hazelnuts. Sift the flour into a mixing bowl with the nuts, sugar, salt, butter and egg yolks and knead together to make a soft dough. Wrap in foil or cling film and leave for 2 hours in the refrigerator.

Form the dough a little at a time into small rolls the thickness of a pencil. Cut the rolls into 5-cm/2-in long pieces and curve them into crescents. Bake in the centre of a moderately hot oven (190 C, 375 F, Gas 5) for 10 minutes until golden. Mix the vanilla sugar with the sifted icing sugar and toss the biscuits in this while still warm.

Rum macaroons

(Illustrated on opposite page)

Cooking temperature moderate
(180 C, 350 F, Gas 4)
Cooking time 15 minutes

50 g/2 oz butter
50 g/2 oz caster sugar
225 g/8 oz ground almonds
4 egg yolks
grated rind of $\frac{1}{2}$ lemon
2 tablespoons rum
few drops of almond essence
DECORATION
glacé cherries or blanched almonds

Grease a baking tray. Beat the butter with the sugar until pale and creamy. Stir in the almonds, egg yolks, lemon rind, rum and almond essence. Place the mixture in an icing bag fitted with a large star nozzle and pipe swirls or stars on the prepared baking tray.

Alternatively, roll the mixture into small balls about the size of a walnut, place them on the baking tray and flatten them slightly with a fork. Top the macaroons with halved glacé cherries or blanched almonds and bake them in a moderate oven (180 C, 350 F, Gas 4) until golden – about 15 minutes. Cool on a wire rack.

Iced pretzels

(Illustrated on opposite page)

Cooking temperature moderate
(180 C, 350 F, Gas 4)
Cooking time 12–15 minutes

200 g/7 oz butter
100 g/4 oz icing sugar
1 egg yolk
pinch of salt
few drops of vanilla essence
300 g/11 oz plain flour
ICING
1 egg white
3 tablespoons rum
2 teaspoons lemon juice
200 g/7 oz icing sugar

Cream the butter with the sifted icing sugar to a smooth paste, then add the egg yolk, salt and vanilla essence. Sift the flour and knead it into the mixture. Wrap the pastry dough in foil or cling film and leave in the refrigerator for 2 hours. Cut off a small piece of pastry at a time and shape it, leaving the rest of the dough in the refrigerator. Roll each piece in turn until pencil thin to a length of 25 cm/10 in. Shape into a pretzel and place on a baking tray. Bake in a moderate oven (180 C, 350 F, Gas 4) for 12–15 minutes.

Mix the egg white with the rum, lemon juice and sifted icing sugar. Allow the pretzels to cool a little then remove them from the baking tray with a palette knife. Place on a wire rack and brush the tops as thickly as possible with the rum icing.

Raspberry sandwich biscuits

(Illustrated on opposite page)

Cooking temperature moderately hot
(190 C, 375 F, Gas 5)
Cooking time 7–10 minutes

150 g/5 oz butter
100 g/4 oz icing sugar
1 egg yolk
few drops of vanilla essence
225 g/8 oz plain flour
100 g/4 oz ground almonds
100 g/4 oz raspberry jam
icing sugar to dust

Lightly grease a baking tray. Beat the butter with the sugar until pale and soft, add the egg yolk, vanilla essence and stir in the sifted flour and ground almonds to form a dough. Knead lightly then allow the pastry to rest in the refrigerator for 1–2 hours. Roll out the pastry to 3 mm/$\frac{1}{8}$ in thick. Use a 5-cm/2-in fluted pastry cutter to cut out the biscuits. Place them on the prepared baking tray and bake in a moderately hot oven (190 C, 375 F, Gas 5) until lightly browned – about 7–10 minutes. Cool on a wire rack.

Warm the jam and use to sandwich the biscuits in pairs. Sift a little icing sugar over the biscuits.

A selection of fancy biscuits

Chocolate almond biscuits

(Illustrated on page 55)

Cooking temperature moderate
(180 C, 350 F, Gas 4)
Cooking time 10–12 minutes

150 g/5 oz butter
100 g/4 oz caster sugar
grated rind of ½ lemon
100 g/4 oz ground almonds
100 g/4 oz plain flour, sifted
FILLING
100 g/4 oz apricot jam
ICING AND DECORATION
175 g/6 oz plain chocolate
25 g/1 oz butter
2 tablespoons chopped pistachio nuts

Lightly grease a baking tray. Cream the butter with the sugar and lemon rind until pale and soft. Stir in the almonds and flour to form a soft dough. Chill the pastry for 1–2 hours, then knead it lightly. Roll out the pastry to 5 mm/¼ in thick and cut out rectangles measuring 2.5 × 3.5 cm/ 1 × ½ in. Place them on the greased baking tray leaving a small space between each as they may spread during baking. Bake in a moderate oven (180 C, 350 F, Gas 4) until lightly browned – about 10–12 minutes. Cool slightly on the baking tray then transfer them to a wire rack.

Warm the jam and use to sandwich the biscuits together in pairs. Melt the chocolate with the butter in a basin over a saucepan of hot water and spread it over the biscuits. Sprinkle with chopped pistachio nuts and allow to set before serving.

Variation

The chilled biscuit dough may be shaped into a roll measuring about 5 cm/2 in. in diameter. Chill the roll and cut it into 5-mm/¼-in thick slices, place them on a baking tray and cook as above. The biscuits may be sandwiched together as above, or simply coated in melted chocolate before serving.

Ginger hearts

(Illustrated on page 55)

Cooking temperature moderately hot
(190 C, 375 F, Gas 5)
Cooking time 10–15 minutes

100 g/4 oz butter
100 g/4 oz caster sugar
1 egg yolk
pinch of salt
1 teaspoon ginger
50 g/2 oz cornflour
1 teaspoon baking powder
175 g/6 oz plain flour
ICING AND DECORATION
175 g/6 oz plain chocolate
25 g/1 oz butter
2 pieces preserved ginger, sliced

Grease a baking tray. Cream the butter with the sugar and egg yolk until pale and soft. Sift the salt, ginger, cornflour, baking powder and flour together and stir them into the creamed mixture to form a dough. Chill the pastry for 2–3 hours.

Knead lightly and roll out the pastry to 5 mm/¼ in thick. Use a heart-shaped biscuit cutter to cut out the biscuits. Place them on the greased baking tray and bake them in a moderately hot oven (190 C, 375 F, Gas 5) until golden brown – about 10–15 minutes. Allow the ginger biscuits to cool slightly on the baking tray and then transfer them to a wire rack.

Melt the chocolate with the butter in a basin over a saucepan of hot water. Coat the top of the biscuits with chocolate. Cut the ginger into strips and arrange two strips in the shape of a cross on each biscuit. Allow the chocolate to set before serving.

Chequered biscuits (page 58)

Jam rings

(Illustrated on the front cover and page 55)

Cooking temperature moderately hot
(190 C, 375 F, Gas 5)
Cooking time 8–10 minutes

175 g/6 oz butter
100 g/4 oz icing sugar
1 egg
grated rind of ½ lemon
pinch of salt
350 g/12 oz plain flour
FILLING
225 g/8 oz raspberry or apricot jam, warmed
icing sugar to dust

Grease a baking tray. Beat the butter and icing sugar together until pale and creamy. Add the egg, lemon rind and salt and stir in the flour to form a dough. Allow the pastry to rest in the refrigerator for 1–2 hours, then roll out to 3 mm/⅛ in thick. Use a 6-cm/2½-in fluted biscuit cutter to cut out an even number of biscuits.

With a 2.5-cm/1-in cutter cut the middle out of half the biscuits or alternatively use a small heart-shaped cutter. Place all the biscuits on the prepared baking tray and bake in a moderately hot oven (190 C, 375 F, Gas 5) for 8–10 minutes. Allow to cool slightly on the baking tray then transfer them to a wire rack.

Sieve the warm jam and use to sandwich each of the biscuit circles with one of the rings. Spoon any remaining jam into the middle of the biscuits and dust the edges with a little icing sugar.

Piped biscuits

Cooking temperature moderate
(180 C, 350 F, Gas 4)
Cooking time 15–20 minutes

100 g/4 oz butter
75 g/3 oz icing sugar
50 g/2 oz cornflour
3 tablespoons milk
pinch of salt
grated rind of 1 lemon
100 g/4 oz plain flour

Lightly grease a baking tray. Beat the butter with the icing sugar until pale and soft. Beat in the cornflour and milk until the mixture is smooth, then add the salt, lemon rind and flour and beat well. Transfer the mixture to a large piping bag fitted with a large star nozzle and pipe stars or swirls on the prepared baking tray. Chill for 30 minutes then bake the biscuits in a moderate oven (180 C, 350 F, Gas 4) for 15–20 minutes until they are pale golden. Allow the biscuits to cool slightly on the tray then transfer them to a wire rack to cool completely.

Chequered biscuits

(Illustrated on page 57)

Cooking temperature moderately hot
(190 C, 375 F, Gas 5)
Cooking time 10–15 minutes

275 g/10 oz butter, softened
150 g/5 oz icing sugar
pinch of salt
400 g/14 oz plain flour
25 g/1 oz cocoa powder
1 egg white

Grease a baking tray. Beat the softened butter with the sifted icing sugar and salt until pale and creamy. Mix in the sifted flour and divide the dough in half. Knead the sifted cocoa powder into one portion. Wrap both portions in foil or cling film and leave for 2 hours in the refrigerator.

Divide each piece of dough into five portions. Roll out one colour into five long, thin rolls. With the other colour, roll out four pieces into long, thin rolls. Arrange these rolls into a chequerboard design, brushing and sealing with a little beaten egg white. Roll out the remaining portion of dough large enough to wrap around the assembled dough. Seal with beaten egg white, wrap in foil or cling film and chill in the refrigerator until firm, about 1 hour.

Cut the dough into 5-mm/¼-in thick slices, place them on the prepared baking tray and bake for 10–15 minutes. Remove the biscuits with a palette knife and cool on a wire rack.

Family cakes

Lemon sponge cake

Cooking temperature moderately hot
(190 C, 375 F, Gas 5)
Cooking time 50–60 minutes

225 g/8 oz butter or margarine
4 eggs
225 g/8 oz caster sugar
100 g/4 oz cornflour
$\frac{1}{2}$ teaspoon baking powder
grated rind of 1 lemon
$\frac{1}{2}$ teaspoon vanilla essence
ICING
150 g/5 oz icing sugar
2 tablespoons maraschino liqueur
1 tablespoon lemon juice

Grease a 20-cm/8-in cake tin and dust it with a little flour. Melt the butter. Separate one of the eggs and whisk the remaining eggs with the yolk and the sugar until thick and creamy. Whisk the egg white until stiff. Sift the cornflour with the baking powder. Fold the butter, lemon rind and vanilla essence into the yolk mixture, then fold in the egg white. Lastly fold in the cornflour and baking powder and turn the mixture into the prepared tin. Bake the cake in a moderately hot oven (190 C, 375 F, Gas 5) for 50–60 minutes, covering it loosely with a piece of cooking foil if it becomes too dark during cooking.

For the icing, sift the icing sugar into a bowl, then beat in the maraschino liqueur and lemon juice until smooth. Spread the icing over the top of the cake while it is still warm.

Marmalade roll

Cooking temperature hot
(220 C, 425 F, Gas 7)
Cooking time 8–10 minutes

3 eggs
75 g/3 oz caster sugar
75 g/3 oz plain flour
225 g/8 oz orange marmalade
icing sugar to dust

Line and grease a 23 × 33-cm/9 × 13-in swiss roll tin. Whisk the eggs with the sugar until thick, pale and creamy. Sift the flour over the mixture and fold it in lightly. Pour this mixture into the prepared tin, spreading it out evenly. Bake the roll in a hot oven (220 C, 425 F, Gas 7) for 8–10 minutes, then turn it out on to a sheet of greaseproof paper placed on a tea towel. Trim the edges off the cake and spread the marmalade over it. Working quickly, roll it up carefully using the tea towel and greaseproof paper to guide it. Cool the roll on a wire rack and dust it with icing sugar before serving. This cake is best eaten freshly baked.

Daisy cake

(Illustrated on page 61)

Cooking temperature moderately hot
(190 C, 375 F, Gas 5)
Cooking time 50–60 minutes

350 g/12 oz butter
100 g/4 oz ground almonds
6 eggs, separated
grated rind of 1 lemon
few drops of vanilla essence
150 g/5 oz caster sugar
120 g/$4\frac{1}{2}$ oz plain flour
75 g/3 oz cornflour
ICING
150 g/5 oz apricot jam
200 g/7 oz icing sugar
1 tablespoon each of lemon juice and water

Grease a 23-cm/9-in round fluted cake tin and sprinkle with fine breadcrumbs. Preheat the oven to moderately hot (190 C, 375 F, Gas 5).

Cream the softened butter with the ground almonds. Stir in the egg yolks, lemon rind and vanilla essence. Whisk the egg whites until stiff then carefully fold in the sugar. Fold the egg whites into the butter mixture. Sift the flour and cornflour together and fold into the mixture. Turn into the prepared cake tin, smooth the surface and bake in a moderately hot oven (190 C, 375 F, Gas 5) for 50–60 minutes.

Cool on a wire rack, then spread with the warmed apricot jam. Leave to cool and set for 30 minutes. Mix the sifted icing sugar with the lemon juice and water and pour over the cake.

Butter cake

Cooking temperature moderate
(180 C, 350 F, Gas 4)
Cooking time 45–50 minutes

150 g/5 oz butter
150 g/5 oz sugar
6 eggs, separated
pinch of salt
grated rind of $\frac{1}{2}$ lemon
150 ml/$\frac{1}{4}$ pint milk
225 g/8 oz self-raising flour
icing sugar to dust

Grease a Kugelhopf mould or ring mould and dust it with a little flour. Cream the butter with half the sugar until pale and soft. Gradually beat in the egg yolks, salt and lemon rind and stir in the milk. Whisk the egg whites until stiff, then gradually whisk in the remaining sugar until the whites are stiff and glossy. Fold half the egg white into the creamed mixture.

Sift the flour and fold it carefully into the mixture, then finally fold in the remaining egg white. Turn the mixture into the prepared tin and bake it in a moderate oven (180 C, 350 F, Gas 4) for 45–50 minutes. Turn the baked cake out on to a wire rack and leave it to cool. Dust the cake with a little icing sugar before serving.

Honey cake

Cooking temperature moderate
(180 C, 350 F, Gas 4)
Cooking time 1$\frac{1}{4}$–1$\frac{1}{2}$ hours

100 g/4 oz caster sugar
225 g/8 oz clear honey
100 g/4 oz butter
2 large eggs, lightly beaten
grated rind of 1 lemon
2 tablespoons rum
275 g/10 oz plain flour
25 g/1 oz cocoa powder
2 teaspoons baking powder
1 teaspoon mixed spice
100 g/4 oz chopped candied peel
75 g/3 oz ground almonds
225 g/8 oz plain chocolate

Line and grease a 1-kg/2-lb loaf tin. Melt the sugar with the honey and butter and allow it to cool slightly. Stir in the eggs, lemon rind and rum. Sift the flour with the cocoa, baking powder and spice and add to the mixture together with the candied peel and ground almonds. Stir well to combine all the ingredients, then spoon the cake into the prepared loaf tin and bake it in a moderate oven (180 C, 350 F, Gas 4) for 1$\frac{1}{4}$–1$\frac{1}{2}$ hours. Turn the cake out on to a wire rack and allow it to cool completely.

Melt the chocolate in a basin over a saucepan of hot water and spread it over the cake to cover it completely. Allow the chocolate to set before serving. This cake keeps well in an airtight container – it should be stored before the chocolate icing is poured over and will keep for up to 2 weeks.

Apple cake

Cooking temperature moderate
(180 C, 350 F, Gas 4)
Cooking time 1–1$\frac{1}{4}$ hours

225 g/8 oz butter or margarine
225 g/8 oz caster sugar
4 eggs
275 g/10 oz self-raising flour
grated rind of $\frac{1}{2}$ lemon
450 g/1 lb cooking apples, peeled, cored and sliced
DECORATION
100 g/4 oz apricot jam
100 g/4 oz flaked almonds, lightly toasted
icing sugar to dust

Grease a 25-cm/10-in round cake tin and dust it with flour. Cream the butter with the sugar until pale and soft. Gradually beat in the eggs and fold in the flour and the lemon rind. Spoon half of the cake mixture into the tin and arrange the apple slices on top, then cover them with the remaining cake mixture. Lightly smooth the top and bake the cake in a moderate oven (180 C, 350 F, Gas 4) for 1–1$\frac{1}{4}$ hours. Cool the apple cake on a wire rack.

Warm and sieve the apricot jam and spread it over the top of the cake. Sprinkle the almonds over and dust it with icing sugar before serving.

Daisy cake (page 59)

Swiss carrot cake

(Illustrated on opposite page)

Cooking temperature moderately hot
(190 C, 375 F, Gas 5)
Cooking time 45–55 minutes

5 eggs, separated, plus 2 egg yolks
200 g/7 oz caster sugar
pinch each of salt, ground cinnamon and
ground cloves
1 tablespoon Kirsch
200 g/7 oz finely grated carrots
100 g/4 oz ground almonds
100 g/4 oz hazelnuts, finely chopped
50 g/2 oz fresh white breadcrumbs
50 g/2 oz plain flour
1 teaspoon baking powder
ICING AND DECORATION
200 g/7 oz icing sugar
2 tablespoons Kirsch
2 tablespoons lemon juice
2 tablespoons apricot jam
50 g/2 oz toasted flaked almonds
100 g/4 oz almond paste
few drops of orange food colouring
few pistachio nut pieces

Grease a 25-cm/10-in springform cake tin. Whisk all the egg yolks with the sugar, salt, cinnamon, cloves and Kirsch until thick and creamy. Mix together the carrots, ground almonds, hazelnuts, breadcrumbs and the flour sifted with the baking powder. Stir these ingredients into the egg yolk mixture.

Whisk the egg whites until stiff and fold in. Turn the cake mixture into the prepared tin, smooth over and bake in a moderately hot oven (190 C, 375 F, Gas 5) for 45–55 minutes. Turn the cake out on a wire rack to cool, cover and leave it for 2 days.

Mix the sifted icing sugar with the Kirsch and lemon juice, and use to ice the top of the cake. Brush the sides of the cake with a little warmed jam and press on the flaked almonds. Colour the almond paste and shape into small carrots. Insert a couple of pistachio nut pieces into one end to resemble the carrot's stalk, and arrange on top of the cake.

Orange cake

(Illustrated on page 65)

Cooking temperature moderate
(160 C, 325 F, Gas 3)
Cooking time 1½–1¾ hours

250 g/9 oz butter or margarine
250 g/9 oz sugar
3 eggs
4 egg yolks
100 g/4 oz self-raising flour
2 teaspoons baking powder
pinch of salt
100 g/4 oz cornflour
2 tablespoons Cointreau
grated rind of 2 oranges
grated rind of 1 lemon
2 tablespoons orange juice
1 tablespoon lemon juice
100 g/4 oz candied orange peel, finely chopped
100 g/4 oz ground almonds
DECORATION
100 g/4 oz orange jelly marmalade
50 g/2 oz flaked almonds, toasted

Grease a 1-kg/2-lb loaf tin and dust it with a little flour. Cream the butter with the sugar until pale and soft. Gradually beat in the eggs and the egg yolks, occasionally adding a spoonful of the measured flour to prevent the mixture from curdling. Sift the flour, baking powder, salt and cornflour together and carefully fold into the creamed mixture. Fold in the Cointreau, fruit rinds and juice and candied orange peel, then lastly fold in the ground almonds. Turn the mixture into the prepared tin and lightly smooth the top.

Bake the cake in a moderate oven (160 C, 325 F, Gas 3) for 1½–1¾ hours, covering the cake loosely with a piece of cooking foil if it becomes too dark during cooking. Turn out the cake and cool it on a wire rack.

Warm the orange jelly marmalade and spread it thinly over the cake, then press the flaked almonds on to the top and sides before serving.

Swiss carrot cake

Pistachio cake

**Cooking temperature moderate
(180 C, 350 F, Gas 4)
Cooking time 1–1¼ hours**

100 g/4 oz pistachio nuts, ground
3 tablespoons rum
100 g/4 oz marzipan
225 g/8 oz butter or margarine
225 g/8 oz caster sugar
5 eggs, separated
pinch of salt
½ teaspoon vanilla essence
175 g/6 oz self-raising flour
100 g/4 oz cornflour
1 teaspoon baking powder
DECORATION
100 g/4 oz plain chocolate
25 g/1 oz butter
1 tablespoon chopped pistachio nuts

Grease a Balmoral tin or 1-kg/2-lb loaf tin and dust with a little flour. Knead the pistachio nuts and 2 tablespoons of the rum into the marzipan and roll it out to approximately 1 cm/½ in thick, then cut it into small cubes.

Cream the butter with half the sugar until soft and pale and gradually beat in the egg yolks, salt, remaining rum and vanilla essence. Whisk the egg whites until stiff, then whisk in the remaining sugar until stiff and glossy.

Fold the egg whites into the butter mixture. Sift the flour with the cornflour and baking powder and fold it into the mixture together with the marzipan cubes. Turn the cake into the prepared tin and bake it in a moderate oven (180 C, 350 F, Gas 4) for 1–1¼ hours until risen, golden brown and firm to touch. Cool the cake on a wire rack.

Melt the chocolate and butter together in a basin over a saucepan of hot water, stir it lightly and spread it over the cooled cake. Sprinkle with chopped pistachio nuts and allow the chocolate to set before serving.

Variation

Ground hazelnuts or walnuts may be substituted for the pistachio nuts. Decorate the cake with a few lightly toasted, chopped whole nuts.

Marble cake

(Illustrated on opposite page)

**Cooking temperature moderately hot
(200 C, 400 F, Gas 6)
Cooking time 60–70 minutes**

2 tablespoons dry white breadcrumbs
100 g/4 oz butter or margarine
150 g/5 oz caster sugar
grated rind of ½ lemon
2 large eggs
150 ml/¼ pint milk
50 g/2 oz cornflour
200 g/7 oz plain flour
1 teaspoon baking powder
25 g/1 oz cocoa powder
icing sugar to dust

Grease a 19-cm/7½-in fluted savarin tin. Sprinkle in the breadcrumbs and tilt the tin to coat the sides. Cream the butter with 100 g/4 oz of the caster sugar and the lemon rind until light and fluffy. Add the eggs, one at a time, with a little of the milk and beat well. Sieve the cornflour, flour and baking powder into the bowl and fold into the creamed mixture with all but 2 tablespoons of the remaining milk.

Spoon half the mixture into the tin. Add the cocoa powder and remaining caster sugar to the other half and mix well with the remaining milk. Spoon into the tin over the plain mixture, and stir gently with a knife into spirals. Bake in a moderately hot oven (200 C, 400 F, Gas 6) for 60–70 minutes or until a skewer inserted in the cake comes out clean. Turn the cake out on to a wire rack. Leave to cool, then sprinkle with icing sugar.

Top: Marble cake;
Bottom right: Orange cake (page 63)

Chocolate Balmoral cake

(Illustrated below)

**Cooking temperature moderate
(180 C, 350 F, Gas 4)
Cooking time 50–60 minutes**

---

100 g / 4 oz butter
100 g / 4 oz caster sugar
100 g / 4 oz plain chocolate
6 eggs, separated
100 g / 4 oz ground almonds
50 g / 2 oz sweet biscuit crumbs
75 g / 3 oz plain flour
DECORATION
100 g / 4 oz plain chocolate
25 g / 1 oz butter
50 g / 2 oz slivered almonds

Grease a Balmoral cake tin or 1-kg/2-lb loaf tin
and dust it with a little flour. Cream the butter
and sugar together until pale and soft. Melt the
chocolate in a basin over a saucepan of hot water
and beat it into the creamed mixture together with
the egg yolks. Whisk the egg whites until stiff and
fold half of them into the creamed mixture. Fold
in the ground almonds, biscuit crumbs and flour
followed by the remaining egg white. Transfer
this mixture to the prepared tin and bake it in a
moderate oven (180 C, 350 F, Gas 4) for 50–60
minutes, then turn it out and cool on a wire rack.

Melt the chocolate with the butter in a basin over
a saucepan of hot water. Press the almonds into
the cake and coat it completely with the melted
chocolate.

Left: Chocolate Balmoral cake;
Right: Linzertorte

Traditional fruit loaf

Cooking temperature moderate
(180 C, 350 F, Gas 4)
Cooking time 1 hour 10 minutes

2 tablespoons milk
4 tablespoons water
1 teaspoon oil
1 teaspoon dried yeast
2 tablespoons lukewarm water
1 teaspoon caster sugar
2 teaspoons salt
50 g/2 oz strong plain flour
50 g/2 oz rye flour
75 g/3 oz dried stoned prunes
175 g/6 oz dried pears
75 g/3 oz dried figs
50 g/2 oz raisins
50 g/2 oz currants
50 g/2 oz chopped candied peel
300 ml/½ pint hot black tea
50 g/2 oz sugar
½ teaspoon ground cinnamon
pinch each of ground cloves, ground aniseed
and salt
2 tablespoons rum
2 tablespoons lemon juice
200 g/7 oz plain flour
50 g/2 oz hazelnuts, finely chopped
DECORATION
25 g/1 oz blanched almonds, halved
glacé cherries
angelica

First make the starter dough. Combine the milk, 4 tablespoons water and the oil in a saucepan and bring to the boil. Allow to cool until lukewarm. Blend the yeast with the lukewarm water and the sugar and leave for 5 minutes. Add to the milk mixture with the salt. Stir this liquid into the plain and rye flour until well blended. Cover and leave to stand for 12–18 hours.

Grease a 20-cm/8-in cake tin with butter or margarine. Chop the prunes, pears and figs. Place them in a bowl with the raisins, currants and candied peel. Pour on the freshly made tea, cover and leave to soak overnight. Add the sugar, spices, salt, rum and lemon juice to the fruit. Stir all the ingredients well, cover and leave to stand for a further 30 minutes.

Add the fruit mixture to the starter dough with the sifted flour and chopped nuts. Mix all thoroughly until well combined and place in the prepared cake tin. Decorate with almond halves, glacé cherries and strips of angelica. Bake in a moderate oven (180 C, 350 F, Gas 4) for 1 hour 10 minutes.

Linzertorte

(Illustrated on opposite page)

Cooking temperature moderately hot
(190 C, 375 F, Gas 5)
Cooking time 35–40 minutes

200 g/7 oz butter or margarine
200 g/7 oz caster sugar
3 eggs
pinch each of salt and ground cloves
½ teaspoon cinnamon
grated rind of ½ lemon
100 g/4 oz sweet biscuit crumbs
150 g/5 oz ground almonds
1 tablespoon plain flour
225 g/8 oz apricot jam
icing sugar to dust

Grease a 25-cm/10-in springform cake tin. Cream the butter and sugar together until pale and soft. Gradually beat in the eggs, salt, ground cloves, cinnamon and lemon rind. Mix the biscuit crumbs and the almonds together and stir them into the creamed mixture to form a soft dough. Chill until firm, then knead the dough lightly and roll out two-thirds of it to line the base of the tin and form a 1.5-cm/¾-in high edge. Knead the flour into the remaining dough and let it rest in the refrigerator for 10 minutes.

Spread the apricot jam over the dough-lined tin. Roll out the remaining dough and cut it into 1-cm/½-in wide strips. Arrange these in a lattice pattern over the jam and bake the Linzertorte in a moderately hot oven (190 C, 375 F, Gas 5) for 35–40 minutes. Leave the cake to cool in the tin then carefully turn it out and dust it lightly with icing sugar before serving.

Biscuit cake

(Illustrated below)

450 g/1 lb plain sweet biscuits
350 g/12 oz butter, melted
½ teaspoon vanilla essence
150 ml/¼ pint single cream
100 g/4 oz plain chocolate
100 g/4 oz ground almonds
1 tablespoon rum
ICING
225 g/8 oz plain chocolate
1 tablespoon rum
50 g/2 oz butter

Grease a 20-cm/8-in loose-bottomed cake tin. Finely crush the biscuits. Melt half the butter and mix it into the biscuit crumbs together with the vanilla essence and cream. Melt the remaining butter with the chocolate in a basin over a saucepan of hot water, then stir in the ground almonds and rum.

Layer these two mixtures together quite thinly in the prepared tin, pressing the biscuits down well. Chill the cake thoroughly for several hours, preferably overnight. Carefully remove the cake from the tin straight on to a serving dish.

To make the icing, melt the chocolate with the rum and butter in a basin over a saucepan of hot water. Spread this over the cake and allow it to set. To cut the cake, use a hot knife.

Suitable for freezing: The layered cake may be frozen in its tin. Defrost the cake slowly in the refrigerator, then turn it out and ice as above.

Biscuit cake

Cream cakes and gâteaux

Fruit layer gâteau

(Illustrated on the front cover and page 71)

Cooking temperature moderately hot
(190 C, 375 F, Gas 5)
Cooking time 40 minutes

4 eggs, separated
2 tablespoons lukewarm water
150 g/5 oz caster sugar
grated rind of $\frac{1}{2}$ lemon
100 g/4 oz plain flour
50 g/2 oz cornflour
1 teaspoon baking powder
FILLING
100 g/4 oz nougat
100 g/4 oz ground almonds
1–2 tablespoons Kirsch
2 tablespoons water
1 tablespoon icing sugar
TOPPING
100 g/4 oz apricot jam
75 g/3 oz toasted flaked almonds
675 g/1$\frac{1}{2}$ lb mixed fruit or 1 (825-g/1 lb 13-oz)
can fruit salad
1 small packet quick-setting jel mix

Grease a 25-cm/10-in springform cake tin. Whisk the egg yolks with the water, half the sugar and the lemon rind, until frothy. Whisk the egg whites until stiff, fold in the remaining sugar, then fold into the egg yolks. Sift the flour with the cornflour and baking powder and fold evenly into the mixture. Turn into the prepared tin and bake in a moderately hot oven (190 C, 375 F, Gas 5) for 40 minutes.

Remove the cake from the tin and cool on a wire rack for at least 2 hours, then cut into three layers.

Melt the nougat in a basin over hot water and spread over one cake layer. Put the next layer on top. Mix the ground almonds with the Kirsch, water and sifted icing sugar and spread over the second layer. Cover with the third cake layer. Spread the top and sides of the cake with the warmed apricot jam and cover the sides with flaked almonds, pressing them on well. Arrange the prepared and drained fruit over the top of the cake and glaze with the jel mix, made up according to the packet instructions.

Blueberry meringue gâteau

Cooking temperature moderately hot
(190 C, 375 F, Gas 5)
and hot (220 C, 425 F, Gas 7)
Cooking time 30–35 minutes

4 eggs
100 g/4 oz caster sugar
pinch of salt
pinch of cinnamon
few drops of vanilla essence
1 tablespoon rum
100 g/4 oz plain flour
25 g/1 oz fresh breadcrumbs
TOPPING
2 egg whites
100 g/4 oz caster sugar
1 (454-g/1-lb) can blueberries or blackberries

Grease a 25-cm/10-in round cake tin and dust with flour. Whisk the eggs with sugar, salt, cinnamon, vanilla essence and rum until thick and creamy. Sift the flour over the mixture and fold it in carefully, using a metal spoon. Finally fold in the breadcrumbs and turn the mixture into the prepared tin. Cook the cake in a moderately hot oven (190 C, 375 F, Gas 5) for 30–35 minutes ntil golden brown and well risen, then turn it out to cool on a wire rack. Increase the oven temperature to hot (220 C, 425 F, Gas 7).

Whisk the egg whites until stiff, then whisk in the sugar until the meringue is very stiff and glossy. Place the cake on a baking tray, drain the blueberries, arrange them on top of the cake and cover it with the meringue, swirled into soft peaks. Return the gâteau to the oven and cook it for 3 minutes until the meringue is lightly browned. Serve immediately.

Variation

To make a baked alaska pudding top the sponge base with a layer of vanilla ice cream and chill it thoroughly in the freezer for about 30 minutes. Make the meringue topping and cover the cake completely with it. Brown the meringue as above and serve immediately.

Mocha meringue gâteau

Cooking temperature very cool
(110 C, 225 F, Gas ¼)
Cooking time 6–10 hours

4 egg whites
225 g/8 oz caster sugar
15 g/½ oz cornflour
MOCHA CREAM
2 teaspoons instant coffee
1 tablespoon cocoa powder
2–3 tablespoons boiling water
300 ml/½ pint double cream
25 g/1 oz icing sugar
cocoa powder to dust (optional)

Line two baking trays with non-stick paper, mark a 25-cm/10-in circle on each and lightly grease them. Whisk the egg whites until stiff and gradually whisk in the sugar until the meringue is very stiff and glossy. Sift the cornflour and carefully fold it into the egg white. Spread this mixture within the marked circles on the paper and place the trays in a very cool oven (110 C, 225 F, Gas ¼) for 6–10 hours. If possible the oven door should be left slightly ajar to allow any steam to escape.

To make the mocha cream, dissolve the coffee and cocoa powder in the boiling water, then stir it into the cream together with the icing sugar and whip it until it stands in stiff peaks. Spread the cream over one meringue layer and place the second layer on top. The top of the meringue may be dusted with a little cocoa powder if liked.

Variation

To make a fruit-filled meringue gâteau, prepare and bake the meringue as above. Fill it with a generous layer of whipped cream and fresh fruit, for example peeled, stoned and sliced peaches, strawberries or raspberries.

Brandy snap garland

(Illustrated on page 73)

Cooking temperature moderate
(180 C, 350 F, Gas 4)
Cooking time 45–60 minutes

175 g/6 oz butter or margarine
175 g/6 oz caster sugar
3 eggs
grated rind and juice of ½ lemon
75 g/3 oz cornflour
1 teaspoon baking powder
150 g/5 oz self-raising flour
FILLING AND ICING
175 g/6 oz butter
350 g/12 oz icing sugar, sifted
1 egg yolk
DECORATION
6–8 brandy snaps, crushed
150 ml/¼ pint double cream
8 glacé cherries, halved

Grease a 23-cm/9-in ring tin. Cream the butter or margarine with the sugar until pale and soft. Gradually beat in the eggs, lemon rind and juice. Sift the cornflour with the baking powder and self-raising flour and fold it into the creamed mixture. Spoon the cake mixture into the prepared tin and bake it in a moderate oven (180 C, 350 F, Gas 4) for 45–60 minutes until well risen and golden brown. Cool the cake slightly in the tin and then turn it out to cool on a wire rack.

To make the filling and icing, cream the butter with the icing sugar and egg yolk until soft and fluffy. Cut the cake into five layers and sandwich it back together with a little of the cream. Spread the remaining cream all over the cake and press on the crushed brandy snaps to cover it completely. Whip the double cream until stiff and place it in a piping bag fitted with a star nozzle. Pipe small swirls of cream around the top of the cake and top each with a halved glacé cherry.

Fruit layer gâteau (page 69)

Viennese chocolate cake

(Illustrated below)

**Cooking temperature moderate
(180 C, 350 F, Gas 4)
Cooking time 50–60 minutes**

---

6 eggs, separated
1 tablespoon vanilla sugar
pinch of salt
150 g/5 oz caster sugar
100 g/4 oz plain chocolate, grated
100 g/4 oz biscuit crumbs
100 g/4 oz ground hazelnuts
FILLING
3 tablespoons sherry
300 g/11 oz apricot jam
ICING
100 g/4 oz plain chocolate
1 egg
200 g/7 oz icing sugar
50 g/2 oz butter

Grease the base of a 25-cm/10-in springform cake tin. Whisk the egg yolks, vanilla sugar, salt and sugar together until pale and creamy. Stir in the grated chocolate. Whisk the egg whites until stiff and fold carefully into the yolk mixture. Mix the biscuit crumbs with the hazelnuts and fold in. Turn into the tin, and bake in a moderate oven (180 C, 350 F, Gas 4) for 50–60 minutes. Turn the cake out on to a wire rack and cool.

Cut the cake through twice to make three layers and soak each layer with sherry. Soften the jam and use to sandwich the layers together.

Melt the chocolate in a basin over a pan of hot water and allow to cool a little. Stir in the egg and sifted icing sugar. Melt the butter and add this to the chocolate, beating well until the mixture is creamy. Cover the top and sides of the cake with this and use a palette knife to swirl the icing. Allow the icing to set before cutting the cake.

Viennese chocolate cake

Prince Regent cake

**Cooking temperature hot
(220 C, 425 F, Gas 7)
Cooking time 5–7 minutes**

7 eggs, separated
150 g / 5 oz caster sugar
pinch of salt
150 g / 5 oz self-raising flour
FILLING
300 ml / ½ pint milk
25 g / 1 oz cornflour
50 g / 2 oz caster sugar
1 egg yolk
250 g / 9 oz butter
50 g / 2 oz plain chocolate
50 g / 2 oz cocoa powder
ICING
200 g / 7 oz plain chocolate

Grease and flour three baking trays. Whisk the egg yolks with half the sugar and the salt until thick. Whisk the egg whites until stiff, whisk in the remaining sugar and fold into the yolks. Sift the flour over the mixture and fold in. Spread the sponge mixture into six 25-cm/10-in rounds on the baking trays and bake in a hot oven (220 C, 425 F, Gas 7) for 5–7 minutes. Cool on wire racks.

Mix a little of the milk with the cornflour. Heat the remaining milk with the sugar and pour on to the cornflour. Return to the heat and bring to the boil, stirring. Add the egg yolk and allow to cool. Cream the butter until soft and then beat it, a spoonful at a time, into the cooled cornflour sauce.

Melt the chocolate in a basin over hot water and add it to the butter cream with the sifted cocoa powder. Spread over the rounds, placing one on top of the other, and use the remainder to cover the top and sides of the cake. Leave in the refrigerator until the cream has set.

Melt the chocolate for the icing and pour over the cake, smoothing with a palette knife.

Below : Brandy snap garland (page 70)

Cherry gâteau

Cooking temperature very cool
(110 C, 225 F, Gas $\frac{1}{4}$)
and moderately hot (190 C, 375 F, Gas 5)
Cooking time 6–7 hours

2 egg whites
100 g/4 oz caster sugar
50 g/2 oz ground almonds
1 tablespoon flour
SPONGE
4 eggs
100 g/4 oz caster sugar
100 g/4 oz plain flour
25 g/1 oz butter, melted
FILLING
150 g/5 oz butter
100 g/4 oz icing sugar
2 egg yolks
2 tablespoons cherry brandy
SYRUP
4 tablespoons water
2 tablespoons sugar
2 tablespoons cherry brandy
DECORATION
50 g/2 oz blanched almonds, chopped
25 g/1 oz icing sugar

Line a baking tray with non-stick paper and mark out a 25-cm/10-in circle on it. Grease the paper and a 25-cm/10-in loose-bottomed cake tin. To make the meringue, whisk the egg whites until stiff, then whisk in the sugar until it is stiff and very glossy. Carefully fold in the ground almonds and flour then spread the mixture within the circle marked on the baking tray. Dry out the meringue in a very cool oven (110 C, 225 F, Gas $\frac{1}{4}$) for 5–6 hours, leaving the oven door slightly ajar so that any steam can escape.

To make the sponge, whisk the eggs and sugar together until pale and thick. Sift the flour and carefully fold it into the mixture together with the butter. Turn the mixture into the prepared cake tin and bake it in a moderately hot oven (190 C, 375 F, Gas 5) for 30–40 minutes. Turn the sponge out to cool on a wire rack.

To make the filling, beat the butter with the icing sugar and egg yolks until pale and creamy. Lastly stir in the cherry brandy. Spread half of this cream over the meringue base, then place the sponge on top. Bring the water and sugar for the syrup to the boil, remove it from the heat and add the cherry brandy. Allow to cool a little, then spoon it over the sponge base ensuring that it all soaks in. Cover the gâteau completely with the remaining cream filling and lastly press the chopped almonds on to the sides. Sift a thick layer of icing sugar over the top and use a large knife to mark a trellis pattern on it. The gâteau tastes best if it is allowed to stand for 2–3 hours before serving.

Sachertorte

Cooking temperature moderate
(180 C, 350 F, Gas 4)
Cooking time 45–60 minutes

150 g/5 oz plain chocolate
150 g/5 oz butter
200 g/7 oz caster sugar
pinch each of salt, cinnamon and grated lemon rind
6 eggs, separated
150 g/5 oz plain flour
FILLING
100 g/4 oz apricot jam
ICING
225 g/8 oz icing sugar
3–4 tablespoons whipping cream
1–2 tablespoons water
75 g/3 oz plain chocolate

Grease a 20-cm/8-in loose-bottomed cake tin and sprinkle it with a little flour. Melt the chocolate in a basin over a saucepan of hot water. Cream the butter with half the sugar, the salt, cinnamon and lemon rind until pale and soft, then gradually beat in the egg yolks and melted chocolate. Whisk the egg whites until stiff and whisk in the remaining sugar until the mixture is stiff and very glossy.

Gently fold first the egg whites and then the flour into the creamed mixture. Turn the mixture into the prepared tin and bake it in a moderate oven (180 C, 350 F, Gas 4) for 45–60 minutes. Turn the cake out on to a wire rack and when completely cooled cut it horizontally into two layers. Sandwich the layers together with the apricot jam.

To make the icing, beat the icing sugar with the water and cream to give a very creamy icing. Melt the chocolate in a basin over a saucepan of hot water and stir into the icing. Spread it over the top of the cake immediately as it sets quickly. Serve the cake when the icing has set.

Peach cream gâteau (page 76)

Peach cream gâteau

(Illustrated on page 74)

Cooking temperature moderately hot
(190 C, 375 F, Gas 5)
Cooking time 30–40 minutes

4 eggs
100 g/4 oz caster sugar
grated rind of 1 lemon
100 g/4 oz plain flour, sifted
FILLING
3 egg yolks
150 ml/¼ pint milk
100 g/4 oz sugar
grated rind of ½ lemon
15 g/½ oz gelatine
3 tablespoons hot water
2 tablespoons Grand Marnier
225 g/8 oz cream cheese
6 fresh peaches or 1 (425-g/15-oz) can sliced
peaches, drained
600 ml/1 pint whipping cream
DECORATION
1 teaspoon chopped pistachio nuts
25 g/1 oz flaked almonds, lightly toasted

Grease a 25-cm/10-in loose-bottomed cake tin and dust it with flour. Whisk the eggs with the sugar until thick and creamy. Fold in the lemon rind and flour. Turn the mixture into the prepared tin and bake it in a moderately hot oven (190 C, 375 F, Gas 5) for 35–40 minutes until well risen and golden brown. Turn the cake out and cool it on a wire rack.

To make the filling, whisk the egg yolks with the milk, sugar and lemon rind in a basin over a pan of hot water until thickened. Dissolve the gelatine in the hot water in a basin over a saucepan of hot water. Stir the dissolved gelatine into the custard, add the Grand Marnier and gradually beat it into the cream cheese. Chill this mixture until set.

Peel the peaches. Cover them with boiling water and leave them to stand for 2–3 minutes, when they can be easily peeled. Halve, stone and evenly slice the peaches then reserve some of the slices for decoration.

Slice the cake horizontally into two layers. Arrange the peach slices on the base, spread the filling over and place the second piece of cake on top. Whip the cream and spread a thin layer of it all over the cake. Pipe a border around the cake and decorate with the reserved peach slices and nuts.

Orange gâteau

(Illustrated on opposite page)

Cooking temperature moderately hot
(190 C, 375 F, Gas 5)
Cooking time 30–40 minutes

4 eggs
100 g/4 oz caster sugar
100 g/4 oz plain flour
grated rind of 1 lemon
FILLING
3 egg yolks
75 g/3 oz caster sugar
100 ml/4 fl oz dry white wine
grated rind and juice of 2 oranges
grated rind and juice of ½ lemon
15 g/½ oz gelatine
2 tablespoons hot water
DECORATION
450 ml/¾ pint double cream
50 g/2 oz flaked almonds, lightly toasted
4 orange slices, quartered

Grease a 20-cm/8-in loose-bottomed cake tin or springform tin and sprinkle it with a little flour. Whisk the eggs with the sugar until thick and creamy. Sift the flour over the mixture and fold it in together with the lemon rind. Turn the mixture into the prepared tin and bake it in a moderately hot oven (190 C, 375 F, Gas 5) for 30–40 minutes. Turn out the cake and cool it on a wire rack.

To make the filling, whisk the egg yolks with the sugar until thick and creamy, gradually stir in the wine, fruit rinds and juices and whisk over a saucepan of hot water until it thickens slightly. Dissolve the gelatine in the hot water, then stir it into the cooled egg mixture. Leave the filling until half set. Cut the cake horizontally into three layers. Place the base in the cake tin and spoon half of the filling over it. Gently lower the middle layer on top and cover with the remaining filling. Top with the third piece of cake and chill until set. Carefully turn the cake out of the tin and place it on a serving dish.

Whip the cream until stiff and spread a thin layer of it over the cake. Mark the top into portions and sprinkle with the flaked almonds, pressing a few around the sides. Place the remaining cream in a piping bag fitted with a star nozzle and pipe swirls of cream around the edge. Top each swirl with a piece of orange before serving.

Orange gâteau

Index